instant
small group

Also by Mike Nappa

Bore No More
The Prayer of Jesus

># instant
small group

52 Sessions
for Anytime,
Anywhere Use

mike nappa

BakerBooks

a division of Baker Publishing Group
Grand Rapids, Michigan

Published by Baker Books
a division of Baker Publishing Group
P.O. Box 6287, Grand Rapids, MI 49516-6287
www.bakerbooks.com

Printed in the United States of America

Library of Congress Cataloging-in-Publication Data
Nappa, Mike, 1963–
    Instant small group : 52 sessions for anytime, anywhere use / Mike Nappa.
        p.   cm.
    Includes bibliographical references and index.
    ISBN 978-0-8010-7281-9 (pbk.)
    1. Bible—Study and teaching. 2. Theology, Doctrinal—Study and teaching.
3. Christian life—Study and teaching. I. Title. II. Title: 52 sessions for anytime, anywhere use. III. Title: Fifty-two sessions for anytime, anywhere use.
BS600.3.N37 2011
230—dc22   2011000973

This book is published in association with Nappaland Literary Agency, an independent agency dedicated to publishing works that are: Authentic. Relevant. Eternal. Visit us on the web at: NappalandLiterary.com

11   12   13   14   15   16   17   7   6   5   4   3   2   1

For Rob Strouse and Jennifer Hanes,
who made me ask a few questions.

Wisdom begins in wonder.

Socrates

contents

7

introduction

The Secret

It doesn't take a genius to lead a small group.

Seriously.

Now, I know that some of my colleagues in professional ministry will take offense at that statement. They're usually the ones who believe the Bible should only be taught by trained professionals—you know, seminarians, Christian counselors, pastors, authors, and the like.

Personally, I think that's a bunch of excrement left behind at a bullfight. (And yes, I've stepped in that excrement more than once in my life!)

After thirty years in both professional and volunteer ministry, I've discovered the secret about what it really takes to lead a powerful, life-changing Bible study group. There are only three things you must have, and they are:

1. You.
2. A Bible.
3. Enough curiosity to ask questions.

Ta-da! You're ready to lead.

Now, if you'd like a little help with number three on that list, then I've got good news for you. This book is going to help you become a person who can comfortably ask relevant, thought-provoking, and sometimes entertaining questions during a small group discussion. Anytime. Anywhere.

Seriously.

Instant Small Group is your pocket-sized teaching resource that provides a year's worth of engaging, transforming, and easy-to-lead discussion guides for adult small groups.

Combining biblical depth with entertaining, educationally sound Socratic teaching techniques, this book will both challenge and inspire members of your small group toward authentic spiritual growth.

All fifty-two guides here require *zero* pre-session preparation—you can literally "open and go" when it's time to begin discussion with your small group. And *anyone* in the group can lead. You can even let group members take turns leading from week to week, lessening the pressure on you to constantly direct the meeting.

Even better—*Instant Small Group* is as transferable as the title suggests. You can use this book in a variety of settings outside the formal small group. For instance, on a road trip, during a retreat, in a coffeehouse, on a date, during dinner with family, as a personal devotional, or even when you're just hanging out with friends.

And here's a little bonus for you: special callouts with discussion-specific teaching tips, brief "Backseat Bible" info, and add-on ideas to enhance the experience are also included. There's even a "Twenty Tips for Dynamic Discussions" appendix at the end of the book that'll give you expert advice for getting the most out of each small group session.

So, no, you don't have to go to seminary to lead an unforgettable small group study at your home or church. And you don't have to be a bona fide member of Mensa or some kind of "professional" Christian either.

All it takes is you, that Bible we mentioned earlier, and a few good questions (your own, or the ones in this book).

So, what are you waiting for?

how to use this book

Congratulations! You are about to have eternal impact by leading these small group discussions with this unique Bible study for adults.

And you're going to have fun doing it!

Here's what you need to know before you begin.

What's a Small Group?

For the purposes of this book, I'm defining a small group as twelve people or less. Generally the discussion sessions work best with at least three people and are designed to work well with up to a dozen folks in the same room. Of course, if you want to adapt this and use it with larger groups (in Sunday school or on a retreat, for example), you can do that too. And you can even work through these discussion guides by yourself as private devotions or Scripture study times if you like—and if you don't mind talking to yourself.

What Kind of Preparation Goes into One of These Sessions?

Hmmm . . . Let's see.
First you open this book to any discussion guide.
Then you start your small group session.

Seriously? That's All It Takes?

Yep. Leading a small group has never been so easy!
Other than a Bible, there are no supplies required. And because each discussion guide includes relevant info about cultural and textual biblical interpretation, no pre-lesson prep is needed either. That way you can discover God's Word together with your group members in fresh, interactive, discussion-starting ways.
If you want to do more, or if you have access to simple supplies (like paper and pencils), I've occasionally included special "Small Group Tip" sections with advice for adding extra elements to a discussion. But really, these are just random add-ons and are not required for your group. All you need is this book and a few Bibles. Oh, and a small group of people who are curious about faith and life.

How Long Are These Portable Discussion Sessions?

Each session in this book runs between thirty and fifty minutes, depending on your group's discussion habits.

What Happens During a Session?

Each discussion guide in this book follows the same structure:

OPEN UP

This is a fun, lighthearted opening question or two to help your group members get to know each other a bit, and to introduce the theme of the session. About 10–15 minutes.

OPEN BOOK

This is the heart of the session. It's where you dig into Scripture, ask the hard questions, and begin to explore how the messages of Scripture relate to your life. About 15–25 minutes.

OPEN LIFE

Here's where you'll both challenge and encourage your group members to take what they've learned so far and let it show up in their life during the coming week. About 5–10 minutes.

Anything Else I Should Know?

Let's see . . .

Expect to see God work among the people in your group through these sessions.

Plan to involve everyone in the discussion.

Don't be afraid to stretch yourself—and those in your group.

Give freedom to disagree.

Challenge people to think for themselves.

Protect the dignity of each individual.

Be aware that silence is OK at times—especially if people are grappling with a challenging question.

Lead by example.

Pray for God to use you and the discussion guides in this book—each and every time.

Oh, and go ahead and have fun. (You're allowed to do that when you're helping to change lives!)

God bless!

discussion
guides
about
christian
essentials

1

God, our father

While he was still a long way off, his father saw him.

Luke 15:20

THEME: **God, our Father**

SCRIPTURE: *Luke 15:11–32; Psalm 68:5–6*

OPEN UP

(10–15 minutes)

1. The nickname committee called! People have so overused traditional father names like "papa," "daddy," and "pops," that the world has almost run out. What are some brand-new nicknames people could use for their fathers during this unexpected shortage? Give an "elevator pitch" for your best idea.

Small Group Tip: *For Extra Fun*

If you have access to paper and pencils, you could also have group members write out their answers to question 1 Hangman-style, with blanks in place of letters for others to guess. This will make small group feel something like a game night, which can be a nonthreatening way to help adults relax and begin to open up with each other.

OPEN BOOK ⬉

(15–25 minutes)

2. The Bible repeatedly describes God as a father. Why is that significant?

Have group members read Luke 15:11–32.

3. What's the first thing that strikes you about the father in this parable? Explain.

4. The father in this passage is an obvious representation of God the Father—and this story was told by Jesus, God's Son. What secrets about the nature of Father God do you see Jesus revealing here?

5. Some say that the father in this parable is passive, permissive, and absent from his son's life—and that God the Father is the same in real life. Do you agree or disagree? Defend your answer.

6. Which is more significant: (a) that the father let the son leave, or (b) that the father welcomed the son back? Explain.

Backseat Bible: *Luke 15:11–32*

According to Jewish custom at the time, by asking for his inheritance early the son in this parable was delivering a terribly harsh insult to his father. He was basically saying, "Dad, I wish you were dead already."[1]

Have group members read Psalm 68:5–6.

7. What's the first thing that strikes you about the Father in this passage? Explain.

8. In what ways does the Father in Psalm 68:5–6 resemble the father in Luke 15:11–32? And why is that important?

24

OPEN LIFE

(5–10 minutes)

9. Think about your current life situation. How do you need God to be your Father today?

10. What are ways that you can "come home" to your heavenly Father this week?

Small Group Tip

Encourage group members to be specific in the way they answer "Open Life" questions. Also, instruct people to wait a minute or two in silence before answering. This will give them an opportunity to think through their responses a bit before having to talk.

Small Group Tip

Consider the option of having group members share their "Open Life" answers with a partner instead of with the whole group. This might be especially helpful if yours is a newly formed small group.

Afterward, have partners pray together in pairs to close the session.

2

Jesus, God's Son

Simon Peter answered, "You are the Christ, the Son of the living God."

Matthew 16:16

THEME: **Jesus, God's Son**
SCRIPTURE: *Matthew 16:13–20; John 1:1–5, 14–18*

OPEN UP

(10–15 minutes)

1. If you were to interview ten people and ask them, "Who is Jesus?" you'd likely get ten different answers. What are ten ways you might expect people to answer that question today?

Small Group Tip: *For Extra Fun*

If you have the time and the courage, send group members out in pairs to a public place (like a mall or outside a coffee shop). Have them actually interview people, asking the question, "In your opinion, who is Jesus?" Have pairs report back on the responses they receive.

(15–25 minutes)

2. Why is it important to decide exactly who Jesus is? Or is it important to do that? Explain.

Have group members read Matthew 16:13–20.

3. What do you think Jesus was trying to accomplish by asking the question he did?

4. At the time Jesus asked this question, there were already many opinions about his identity. Today there is often startling unanimity about historical/religious figures—except Jesus. Why can't anyone seem to agree about him?

5. Jesus clearly indicated that Simon Peter's understanding came to him directly from God. What does that mean for you and me today?

Backseat Bible: *Matthew 16:13*

It's interesting to note that Caesarea Philippi was the place where Jesus stopped to ask "Who do people say the Son of Man is?" That region had only recently been renamed Caesarea Philippi (after its new Roman rulers). For hundreds of years prior, the area had been known as *Panion*, which means "Sanctuary of Pan," a place dedicated to honoring the pagan god associated with nature.

This means that when Jesus asked the question to clarify the truth of his deity in the eyes of his disciples, they were all standing in a centuries-old worship sanctuary of a false god.[2]

Have group members read John 1:1–5, 14–18.

6. Who does John say that Jesus is?

7. John uses terms like "Word," "Life," and "Light" to describe Jesus. How does that help—or hinder—your understanding of Jesus?

8. "Through him all things were made" (v. 3). What does that all-encompassing statement imply about Jesus? How can we know if these implications are true?

OPEN LIFE

(5–10 minutes)

9. As far as you are concerned, who is Jesus?

10. What difference, if any, will that make in your life tomorrow? Why?

Small Group Tip

Consider the option of having group members share their "Open Life" answers with a partner instead of with the whole group. This might be especially helpful if yours is a newly formed small group.

Afterward, have partners pray together in pairs to close the session.

3

the Holy Spirit

The Holy Spirit . . . will teach you all things.

John 14:26

THEME: **The Holy Spirit**

SCRIPTURE: *John 14:16–17, 26; Acts 2:1–13*

OPEN UP

(10–15 minutes)

1. Cover your eyes with your hands. Even though you can't see anything, what do you *know* exists in this room right now? How do you know it?

OPEN BOOK

(15–25 minutes)

2. What exists right now that you can't see, smell, taste, touch, or hear? How do you know it?

Have group members read John 14:16–17, 26.

3. Critics of Christianity doubt the Holy Spirit exists. They assume Christ's promise in John 14 is wishful thinking at best or a lie at worst. How can we know if these critics are right?

4. Jesus promised that his Holy Spirit would: (a) be a Counselor, (b) live *with* you, (c) be *in* you, (d) teach you all things, (e) remind you of everything Jesus said. Has that promise come true in your life? Explain your answer.

5. Jesus never indicated that the Holy Spirit's work was a part-time job. Why is that important? And what causes us to miss the Holy Spirit's full-time presence?

Backseat Bible: *Acts 2:4–11*

One immediate consequence of the Holy Spirit's arrival was that Jesus's disciples began speaking in at least fifteen foreign dialects (vv. 4, 9–11). Some theologians suggest that this miraculous event indicated a symbolic "reversal of the judgment at the Tower of Babel when God confused man's language" (Genesis 11). In other words, at Babel, humankind was forcibly divided. Through the Holy Spirit's redemptive presence, we can be reunited in Christ.[3]

Have group members read Acts 2:1–13.

6. What's your initial reaction after reading this account of the Holy Spirit's coming at Pentecost?

7. At this coming, the presence of the Holy Spirit was accompanied by the sound of violent wind, the sight of fiery images, and miraculous, spontaneous, multilingual testimonies about God. Those three occurrences never happened at the same time again. Why not?

8. What do you think Acts 2 reveals about the Holy Spirit as our Counselor? As our Teacher? As Christ's presence living *with* us and *in* us?

(5–10 minutes)

9. Cover your eyes with your hands. When you can't see, smell, taste, touch, or hear the Holy Spirit, how do you *know* the Holy Spirit is near?

10. What would you like to say to the Holy Spirit right now?

Small Group Tip

Encourage group members to be specific in the way they answer "Open Life" questions. Also, instruct people to wait a minute or two in silence before answering. This will give them an opportunity to think through their responses a bit before having to talk.

4

the spirit realm

Are not all angels ministering spirits?

Hebrews 1:14

THEME: **Angels and Demons**

SCRIPTURE: *Hebrews 1:14; Ephesians 6:10–12*

OPEN UP

(10–15 minutes)

1. If you were a Hollywood producer casting an angel and a demon in a film, whom would you cast in each role? Why?

OPEN BOOK

(15–25 minutes)

2. The Bible clearly assumes that a spiritual realm with both angels and demons exists. Have you ever experienced that realm? If yes, when? If no, does that make you disbelieve in a spiritual realm?

Have group members read Hebrews 1:14.

3. How would you define the term "ministering spirits" as it's used in this Scripture?

4. In what ways do angels seem to serve us today? Be specific.

5. If angels are constantly in God's service on our behalf, then why do bad things happen while they are on the job?

6. Is it appropriate to pray to angels for help? Defend your answer.

Backseat Bible: *Hebrews 1:14*

Almost in passing, Hebrews 1:14 calls angels "ministering spirits" sent to serve. That phrase glosses over the rich history that angels have played in human affairs.

Often pictured in Scripture as something akin to an entourage of heavenly courtiers, angels have fulfilled varied roles that mirror the functions of an earthly royal court. Among other things, angels have acted as messengers (Matt. 1:20–24), instruments of justice (Num. 22:21–33), bodyguards (Exod. 14:19–20), soldiers (2 Kings 19:32–36), and even worshipers (Isa. 6:1–3).[4] As such, they lend credence to the scriptural images of God as the "Great King" and Christ as the "King of kings."

Have group members read Ephesians 6:10–12.

7. What do you feel when you think about a spiritual realm that surrounds and influences your life each day? Describe your emotions.

8. Ephesians 6:10–12 assumes that it is the Christian's responsibility to stand against demonic power in the spiritual realm. What role, if any, do angels play in that?

9. In a realistic, day-to-day sense, what does it mean to "struggle . . . against the spiritual forces of evil" (v. 12)?

OPEN LIFE ➤

10. This week, what questions do you want God to answer for you about angels and demons? How will you seek his answers?

Small Group Tip

Encourage group members to be specific in the way they answer "Open Life" questions. Also, instruct people to wait a minute or two in silence before answering. This will give them an opportunity to think through their responses a bit before having to talk.

5

God's word for us

All Scripture is God-breathed.

2 Timothy 3:16

THEME: **The Bible**

SCRIPTURE: *Psalm 119:105; 2 Timothy 3:16–17*

OPEN UP

(10–15 minutes)

1. Look around the room right now and pick out one common household item. Next, use that item as a comparison to complete this sentence: "God's Word is like [household item] because . . ."

(For instance: "God's Word is like that painting on the wall, because I see something new in it every time I look at it." Or, "God's Word is like that shoe because it helps protect me when I go to new places.")

Small Group Tip: *For Extra Fun*

If your group is feeling rowdy and enthusiastic, the first question works great as a game of charades with teams!

OPEN BOOK

(15–25 minutes)

2. What makes the Bible easy or difficult for you?

Have group members read Psalm 119:105.

3. The psalmist tried to make Scripture easier to understand by comparing it to a common household item: a lamp. Does that description help you? Why or why not?

4. In what ways has God's Word been a lamp or a light for you in the past? Be specific.

5. Psalm 119:105 implies that we are constantly moving in our spiritual lives—and that we need God's Word to light our way as we progress from one place to the next. What kind of spiritual movement do you think the psalmist is referring to?

Backseat Bible: *Psalm 119:105*

In Psalm 119:105 the psalmist uses the imagery of a household lamp to describe God's Word. At this time in ancient Israel, a household lamp was typically a small ceramic bowl filled with oil. A short "nose" at one side of the bowl held a wick (usually a piece of cloth) that extended into the oil.

Interestingly, this type of lamp wasn't known for creating a broad beacon of light suitable for large groups. Rather, this lamp was a personal tool, giving just enough light for one person to see short distances ahead. In that context, when the psalmist says God's Word is "a light for my path," he is creating a visual picture that shows God's Word as necessary, personal help for taking life one step at a time.[5]

Have group members read 2 Timothy 3:16–17.

6. There have been centuries of debate over the term translated "God-breathed" in 2 Timothy 3:16. In the simplest of explanations, what do you think that term means?

7. If God whispered in your ear right now, what would you do? How is that different from the way you react to the God-breathed words in the Bible?

8. In what ways does Psalm 119:105 shed light on the workings of Scripture described in 2 Timothy 3:16–17?

OPEN LIFE

(5–10 minutes)

9. Think about your life right now, and pick one circumstance that makes you feel concerned or even overwhelmed. Next, complete this sentence: "God's Word can equip me for this situation because . . ."

10. How will you take advantage of God's Word each day this week? And who will help you do that?

Small Group Tip

Consider the option of having group members share their "Open Life" answers with a partner instead of with the whole group. This might be especially helpful if yours is a newly formed small group.

Afterward, have partners pray together in pairs to close the session.

6

in the beginning

In the beginning God created.

Genesis 1:1

THEME: **Creation**

SCRIPTURE: *Genesis 1; Colossians 1:15–17*

OPEN UP

(10–15 minutes)

1. In your humble—but accurate!—opinion, what's the greatest thing you've ever created with your own hands?

Small Group Tip: *For Extra Fun*

If you have access to modeling clay, go ahead and toss a chunk to each group member. Then, in response to question 1, have everyone sculpt a model of his or her greatest creation to show off (and explain) to the group.

2. In your humble—but accurate!—opinion, what's the greatest thing God ever created?

Have group members read Genesis 1.

3. For most non-Christians—and even a significant number of Christians—Genesis 1 is just another myth about the beginning of the world. What's your response to that viewpoint?

4. What captures your attention most in this telling of the world's origins? Why?

5. Why is it important to think of the world—and us in it—as being something created by God?

Backseat Bible: *Genesis 1:3–31*

How long is a "day" in Genesis? Scholars have long argued that question. Some have suggested the days in Genesis are figurative, referring to what we now consider the geological ages of earth. Others believe the days in Genesis 1 are merely when God *revealed* his creative work, not the time it took for him to actually create.

Still, in this case, perhaps it's best to let the Bible speak for itself. When Genesis says God fully created certain portions of the world on certain days, the Hebrew word used for "day" in that text is *yôm*. That word is used again several other times in Scripture (for instance, Exod. 20:11). Every time it's used, it means the same thing: A literal, 24-hour period.[6]

Have group members read Colossians 1:15–17.

6. In five words or less, exactly what is Colossians 1:15–17 claiming? How can that be true?

7. Where do you see Christ's fingerprints in creation? Explain.

8. How do you understand the statement in verse 17 that says through Jesus "all things hold together"?

OPEN LIFE

(5–10 minutes)

9. If Jesus did indeed create all things, that means he created all of you: your appearance, your health, your intellect, your DNA, your emotional tendencies, your thought processes, and more. What does that mean to you right now?

10. If Jesus did indeed create all things, that means he created every person you will come into contact with this week. What will that mean to you tomorrow?

Small Group Tip

Encourage group members to be specific in the way they answer "Open Life" questions. Also, instruct people to wait a minute or two in silence before answering. This will give them an opportunity to think through their responses a bit before having to talk.

7

saving us from ourselves

The wages of sin is death.

Romans 6:23

THEME: **Sin and Forgiveness**

SCRIPTURE: *Romans 6:23; 1 John 1:8–9*

OPEN UP

(10–15 minutes)

1. What comes to your mind when you visit a cemetery? Describe it.

Small Group Tip: *For Extra Fun*

If the weather is nice and your group is agreeable, consider holding this meeting on the grounds of a local cemetery. Bring a few blankets and actually sit out among the rows of gravestones while you talk.

OPEN BOOK

(15–25 minutes)

Have group members read Romans 6:23.

2. What comes to your mind when you read Romans 6:23? Describe it.

3. People sin all the time without dying. In what ways do sins actually pay out in death? Be specific.

4. In what ways is a relationship with Jesus a gift of life? Be specific.

5. If we know the truth of Romans 6:23, then why is it easier to indulge in sin on a daily basis than it is to embrace life in Christ on a daily basis? What can be done about that?

Backseat Bible: *Romans 6:23*

In 62 BC, the Roman general Pompey conquered Palestine and dragged many of its residents back to Rome as slaves. Over a century later (around AD 54) children and grandchildren of those Jewish slaves made up a significant portion of the church to which Paul wrote what became the book of Romans. As both foreigners and descendants of slaves, they would have continued to endure harsh oppression and sinful treatment at the hands of Roman soldiers in the city.

This distinction bears new importance when reading Romans 6:23. The word Paul used for "wages" here referred to the pay a soldier received for his military duties. In that context, Romans 6:23 seems to appeal to inherent Jewish longing for judgment of sin, and also to make an inference that even those who are rewarded for sin (i.e., a Roman soldier paid to oppress the innocent) earn sin's terrible, natural payment: death.[7]

Have group members read 1 John 1:8–9.

6. Why would anyone "claim to be without sin"? How do we see that claim show up in both our society and our personal lives?

42

7. If God already knows our sin, why do we need to confess it to him?

8. Obviously, we could never remember to confess every little (or big) sin we commit—yet 1 John 1:9 insists that God forgives "all" sin after we confess. What's the deal with that?

OPEN LIFE ▶

(5–10 minutes)

9. Imagine your left hand represents the "wages of sin," and your right hand represents "eternal life in Christ Jesus." Which hand best represents you right at this moment? Explain.

10. What has to happen for you to experience the truth of 1 John 1:8–9 this week?

Small Group Tip

The topics of sin and forgiveness can sometimes be very personal for group members, so be sure to emphasize—and protect the idea—that your group is a safe environment for sharing.

Also, if there are those in your group who are not yet Christians, the Open Life portion of this session leads toward an opportunity for you to invite a new commitment to Christ. If it seems appropriate, consider taking a moment or two to share your own experience of becoming a follower of Jesus, and asking if anyone in your group would also like to become a Christian. Be sure to follow up individually afterward with anyone who responds.

8

amazing grace

It is by grace you have been saved.

Ephesians 2:8

THEME: **Grace**

SCRIPTURE: *Matthew 20:1–16; Ephesians 2:8–9*

OPEN UP

(10–15 minutes)

1. Is God fair? Explain your answer.

OPEN BOOK

(15–25 minutes)

2. Think of a time when it felt like God was being unfair toward you. What happened?

Have group members read Matthew 20:1–16.

3. What are your thoughts on God's fairness after reading this parable?

4. The landowner in this parable is an obvious representation of God. Do you think it's significant that his generosity (the worker's wage) was only enough for one day? Explain.

5. What are some intangible benefits (emotional, social, personal, etc.) the workers may have received based on what time they began to serve the landowner? What intangible benefits do God's servants receive today?

Backseat Bible: *Matthew 20:1–16*

Jesus's parable of the workers mirrored a well-known Jewish folktale on a similar theme—but with one stark contrast. In the Jewish story, the people of Israel represented those who had worked long and hard in the kingdom of God. At Judgment Day, they would be rewarded with high wages. Non-Jews represented those who came late into God's service. At judgment, they'd be allowed into heaven but would receive little reward.

Jesus, however, turned that thinking on its head. In this parable, he suggested that God intended to be generous toward all—both Jew and non-Jew alike.[8]

Have group members read Ephesians 2:8–9.

6. What light does this Scripture shed on our discussion of the parable in Matthew 20?

7. "By grace . . . through faith." What's the difference?

8. Is the act of faith (choosing to believe and follow Christ) a work of God or a work of the individual? Defend your answer.

OPEN LIFE

(5–10 minutes)

9. How would you explain the difference between expecting God's promise of grace, and demanding God's benefits of grace?

10. What will you do this week to help yourself respond joy-fully to God's grace—no matter how it shows up in your life?

Small Group Tip

Encourage group members to be specific in the way they answer "Open Life" questions. Also, instruct people to wait a minute or two in silence before answering. This will give them an opportunity to think through their responses a bit before having to talk.

9

the faith factor

Faith is being sure.

Hebrews 11:1

THEME: **Faith**

SCRIPTURE: *Hebrews 11:1; John 20:24–29*

OPEN UP ▶

(10–15 minutes)

1. Hold up your purse or wallet. Without looking inside, answer this question: Exactly how much money is in there?

Small Group Tip

If some in your group feel uncomfortable talking about money, you can also change the first question as follows: "Hold up your purse or wallet. Without looking inside, name five specific things that you are certain are in there."

OPEN BOOK

2. What made you feel certain, or uncertain, about your answer to the first question?

Have group members read Hebrews 11:1.

3. This is a pretty demanding definition of faith. What makes you feel certain—or uncertain—about living that kind of faith lifestyle?

4. Is there a difference between "being sure of what we hope for" and hoping for the best? How does that difference play out in real life?

5. Hebrews 11:1 says clearly what faith *is*. Based on that definition, what do you think faith *is not*?

Backseat Bible: *John 20:28*

In the intensely monotheistic society of first-century Judaism, Thomas's exclamation of "My Lord and my God!" would have been considered blasphemy. Why? Because Thomas had just declared that Jesus, the man, was in fact, God. Some have since tried to explain away Thomas's declaration as simply the equivalent of a shocked expletive that inadvertently took God's name in vain. However, that ignores the context of the statement—and the fact that Thomas spoke the words directly to Christ. For Thomas, seeing was obviously believing.[9]

Have group members read John 20:24–29.

6. What's your first impression of Thomas after reading this story?

7. What words might describe the way Thomas felt at the beginning of this experience? In the middle? At the end?

8. How do feelings influence faith?

OPEN LIFE

(5–10 minutes)

9. Hold up your purse or wallet and imagine it holds "coins of faith" (from one cent to ninety-nine cents) inside. Exactly how much "faith money" do you think is in there? Explain.

10. How might remembering Hebrews 11:1 and John 20:24–29 help increase your faith this week?

Small Group Tip: *For Extra Fun*

If you have access to enough coins—pennies, nickels, quarters, etc.—it might be fun to end this session by giving each group member one coin. Tell people to use it as a reminder of the insights about faith you uncovered during your discussion time today.

10

the body of Christ

Every day they continued to meet together.

Acts 2:46

THEME: **The Church**

SCRIPTURE: *Acts 2:42–47; Ephesians 2:19–22*

OPEN UP (10–15 minutes)

1. If you could be famous for anything, what would you want to be known for?

OPEN BOOK (15–25 minutes)

2. If your church were famous worldwide, what do you think it would be known for?

Have group members read Acts 2:42–47.

3. When the church first began, what was it known for? How does that compare to what churches are known for today?

4. What should people expect from a church today?

5. What should a church expect from its people?

Backseat Bible: *Ephesians 2:19–22*

Paul's adamant declaration in Ephesians 2:19–22 that all believers—regardless of race or national origin—were "fellow citizens" and "members of God's household" was both countercultural and dangerous. At the time this was written, Jews and Syrians were embroiled in a bloody race war in nearby Caesarea—a place Paul had actually visited. History records that these people groups massacred each other in brutal, often retaliatory attempts at racial cleansing. As a leading Jew, Paul would have been expected to side with his countrymen. Instead, he sided with Christ.[10]

Have group members read Ephesians 2:19–22.

6. Does your experience with the church confirm Paul's description of it in Ephesians 2:19–22? Why or why not?

7. What part does unity play in Paul's description of "God's household"?

8. What makes it difficult for us to live in unity as "fellow citizens" and "members of God's household"?

OPEN LIFE

(5–10 minutes)

9. What insights from today's discussion do you think are important to remember?

10. How do you think your upcoming week would be different if you prayed each day, "God, give me new passion for your church"? Are you willing to find out?

Small Group Tip

Encourage group members to be specific in the way they answer "Open Life" questions. Also, instruct people to wait a minute or two in silence before answering. This will give them an opportunity to think through their responses a bit before having to talk.

11

praying is believing

Pray continually.

1 Thessalonians 5:17

THEME: **Prayer**

SCRIPTURE: *Matthew 6:9–13; 1 Thessalonians 5:17*

OPEN UP

(10–15 minutes)

1. If prayer were a pie, what ingredients and instructions would the recipe contain?

Small Group Tip: *For Extra Fun*

If your small group likes to cook, why not go ahead and hold this meeting as part of a pie-making extravaganza in the church kitchen? (Be sure to share the results with your church custodian!)

OPEN BOOK ▶

2. What is one thing you wish you knew about prayer? Why?

Have group members read Matthew 6:9–13.

3. What "ingredients" do you see in Jesus's model prayer? What's not in the prayer that you might expect to be there?

4. Do you think it's significant that Jesus began this model prayer by calling God, "Our Father"? Why or why not?

5. Part of this prayer, "Hallowed be your name, your kingdom come" echoes the phrasing of a common Jewish prayer called the *Kaddish*.[11] Was Jesus plagiarizing here? Or was something else going on? Explain your answer.

Backseat Bible: *1 Thessalonians 5:17*

For all his lofty-minded theology, the apostle Paul certainly knew how to ground his teaching in the most basic, practical experiences of life. One excellent example of this is in 1 Thessalonians 5:17. When exhorting his readers to "pray continually," the adverb Paul used was *adialeiptōs*—a Greek word generally associated with a persistent, hacking cough![12]

Have group members read 1 Thessalonians 5:17.

6. How, exactly, does one "pray continually"?

7. What happens when prayer becomes an important, ever-present part of life? Describe it.

8. Some say prayer changes God and prompts him to act on our behalf. Others say God changes us through our prayers, and his answers (or nonanswers) to our requests are only secondary in importance. What do you say?

(5–10 minutes)

9. In your experience, what's been your biggest disappointment in prayer? How did you (do you) respond to that?

10. What can you do tomorrow to deepen your experience in prayer?

Small Group Tip

Encourage group members to be specific in the way they answer "Open Life" questions. Also, instruct people to wait a minute or two in silence before answering. This will give them an opportunity to think through their responses a bit before having to talk.

12

praise power

Praise the LORD.

Psalm 150:1

THEME: **Worship**
SCRIPTURE: *John 4:20–24; Psalm 150*

OPEN UP

(10–15 minutes)

1. If you were not allowed to use words or songs to worship God, what would your praise look like?

Small Group Tip: *For Extra Fun*

If your group is generally uninhibited, one fun way to answer the first question is with pair pantomime. Have one person in each pair act as a statue, and the other as the sculptor. Have the sculptor position his or her "statue" in a posture or expression that somehow represents the pair's answer to the question.

OPEN BOOK ►

2. Using only one word, fill in the blank in this sentence: "When we worship God, _____ happens." Why did you choose that word?

Have group members read John 4:20–24.

3. Jesus indicates that the Father "seeks" worshipers (v. 23). If he's God, and truly self-sustaining in every way, why does he seek people to worship him?

4. What does it really mean to worship God "in spirit and in truth"?

5. Who benefits most from worship, God or us? Explain your answer.

Backseat Bible: *Psalm 150*

Theologian Lawrence O. Richards gives probably the best explanation of praise and worship I've ever read. Listen to how he describes it (italics mine):

> Praise is more than acknowledgment. *It is also an expression of delight.* It is reveling in the God who has shown himself to us. It is expressing the love that wells up within us by speaking to him. . . . When we speak to him, we join with believers through the ages who have expressed their love for the Lord by praising him for his great and wonderful acts and for his great and wonderful self.[13]

Have group members read Psalm 150.

6. What emotions do you see displayed in this psalm?

7. What part do emotions play in healthy praise and worship today? When do emotions become unhealthy in praise and worship?

8. Can you worship God when you don't feel like it? How? And why would you?

OPEN LIFE

9. Which is easier for you: (a) to worship God for what he has done, or (b) to worship God for who he is? Explain.

10. What are seven different ways we can worship Christ in spirit and in truth during this next week? Let's brainstorm now.

Small Group Tip

For question 10, consider having group members first work together in pairs or trios to come up with a few brainstorm ideas to share with the whole group.

13

the last days

Heaven and earth will pass away, but my words will never pass away.

Luke 21:33

THEME: **The Last Days**
SCRIPTURE: *Luke 21:7–17, 32–36*

OPEN UP

(10–15 minutes)

1. What's the best "disaster movie" you've ever seen? What made it so compelling to you?

OPEN BOOK

(15–25 minutes)

2. Why do you suppose people are so often fascinated by end-of-the-world stories?

Have group members read Luke 21:7–17.

3. What do you think prompted Jesus's disciples to ask him for details about the disasters that would precede the end of the world?

4. If you could ask Jesus one question about his predictions in Luke 21:7–17, what would it be? What do you think his answer would be?

5. Some say we are currently in the last days. Others say the last days are still far away. How could you defend either viewpoint in a debate?

Backseat Bible: *Luke 21:7–36*

Some theologians believe Jesus's prophecies in Luke 21 speak of two different, yet intertwined, cataclysmic events: (1) the destruction of Jerusalem, and (2) the destruction of the world at his second coming. This would mirror the way Old Testament prophecies about Christ also often had dual applications. (For instance, messianic prophecies in Psalms 22:6–7; 41:9; and 69:9 described both the life of Israel's King David and the future incarnation of Jesus Christ.)

If this duality of thinking is correct, then the first part of Jesus's prophecy likely occurred in AD 70 when Roman troops leveled Jerusalem—something that would fulfill the generational prediction recorded in Luke 21:32. The second aspect of Jesus's prophecies in Luke 21, regarding his triumphant return, has yet to occur.[14]

Have group members read Luke 21:32–36.

6. What do you think of Jesus's claim (v. 32) that all his predictions would come to pass before that generation passed away? Explain.

7. What is our responsibility in anticipation of the last days that Jesus described? And how exactly does one live out that responsibility among twenty-first century activities like

work, school, parenting, politics, social functions, and even church membership?

8. Would it make a difference in your lifestyle if you knew exactly when the world would end? Why or why not?

OPEN LIFE

(5–10 minutes)

9. "Love like the world ends tomorrow. Live like it ends a hundred years from now. Laugh like it never ends at all." In light of Jesus's words in Luke 21, what's helpful or unhelpful about this saying?

10. Jesus encouraged us to "be always on the watch." How can we help each other do that this week?

Small Group Tip

Encourage group members to be specific in the way they answer "Open Life" questions. Also, instruct people to wait a minute or two in silence before answering. This will give them an opportunity to think through their responses a bit before having to talk.

discussion
guides
about
personal
growth

14

follow the leader

So they . . . left everything and followed him.

Luke 5:11

THEME: **Discipleship**
SCRIPTURE: *Luke 5:1–11; Ephesians 5:1–2*

OPEN UP

(10–15 minutes)

1. The Sign Language Committee called! They're looking for a new hand motion to represent the word "disciple"— what ideas can we suggest for them?

Small Group Tip

For question 1, consider having group members first work together in pairs to come up with a few brainstorm ideas to share with the larger group.

(15–25 minutes)

2. What do you think it means to be a disciple of Jesus?

Have group members read Luke 5:1–11.

3. From what you can tell, what do you think it meant for Simon Peter, James, and John to be disciples of Jesus?

4. How do you explain Simon Peter's initial reaction to Jesus (v. 8)? And how do you explain Jesus's reaction to Simon (v. 10)?

5. Jesus never actually *asked* Simon Peter, James, and John to become his disciples—he appears to assume they'll leave everything and follow him without question. And they did. Why do you suppose that is?

Backseat Bible: *Luke 5:10–11*

The practice of a Jewish rabbi like Jesus teaching a close group of dedicated followers/students (i.e., disciples) was common in first-century Israel. What was uncommon was the way people became disciples of Jesus.

During that time and in that culture, prospective disciples typically took responsibility for choosing their own rabbis. But, as Luke 5:10–11 reveals, Jesus completely reversed that thinking. When it came time for his disciples, Rabbi Jesus chose who would follow him—not vice versa.[1]

Have group members read Ephesians 5:1–2.

6. Ephesians 5:1–2 is often used as a guideline for discipleship. What does it say to you as a follower of Christ in the twenty-first century? Be specific.

7. Our position as God's "dearly loved children" appears to play a central role in our motivation and practice of imitating God. Why do you suppose that's so?

8. The primary characteristic of a disciple is living "a life of love." How does that show up at home? At work? In your community? When you are alone?

OPEN LIFE

(5–10 minutes)

9. What's the best way to balance the lofty call of discipleship (i.e., giving your all in service) with the realities of practical life (limited time, abilities, and resources)?

10. If Jesus walked into this room right now and said, "Follow me," where do you think he'd take you this week? And what would it mean for you to go there?

Small Group Tip

Consider the option of having group members share their "Open Life" answers with a partner instead of with the whole group. This might be especially helpful if yours is a newly formed small group.

Afterward, have partners pray together in pairs to close the session.

15

dealing with disappointment

I have the desire to do what is good, but I cannot carry it out.

Romans 7:18

THEME: **Failure**

SCRIPTURE: *Mark 14:66–72; Romans 7:14–25*

OPEN UP

(10–15 minutes)

1. What's the best advice you've ever heard about failure? Where did you hear it, and how have you used it in your life?

OPEN BOOK

(15–25 minutes)

2. The Bible is filled with accounts of heroes who experienced spectacular failures in matters of faith. Why were those embarrassing stories included in Scripture?

Have group members read Mark 14:66–72.

3. What's your impression of Peter after reading about his failure here?

4. When have you felt like Peter in this situation? What happened?

5. If you had been standing next to Peter at this time, what advice would you have given him afterward?

Backseat Bible: *Romans 7:14–25*

Some think that Paul's description of his struggle with sin in Romans 7 is merely the apostle reflecting on his sinful life prior to becoming a follower of Christ. However, that view misses the clear grammatical shift in Paul's discussion here. Beginning in verse 14 and continuing through the end of the chapter, Paul switches from speaking about theoretical ideas in the past tense to speaking of his *personal experience in the present tense.*[2]

What does that mean? Just that Paul—the great apostle, Christian missionary, theological expert, and actual human author of Scripture—still endured repeated failure in the face of sin's temptation and power even *after* devoting his life to Christ.

Have group members read Romans 7:14–25.

6. How does Paul's experience described in Romans 7:14–25 compare to Peter's experience in Mark 14:66–72?

7. Why do Christians, who are empowered by God's infinite Holy Spirit, continue to struggle with doing what's right?

8. If occasional (or frequent!) failure in the face of sin is inevitable, then what is a Christian's best response to it? How does that apply personally? Toward others?

OPEN LIFE

9. True or false: "Failure is an act, not a person." How do Mark 14:66–72 and Romans 7:14–25 help you answer that true/false question?

10. Imagine that tomorrow you receive a letter with these instructions on the envelope: "To Be Opened in the Event of Failure This Week." Upon closer inspection, you discover the letter is from yourself! What advice do you expect to find in that letter?

Small Group Tip: *For Extra Fun*

If you have access to paper, pencils, and envelopes, have group members write actual letters to themselves as their answers to question 10. Tell everyone to seal their letters in the envelopes and to keep them nearby during the coming week . . . just in case they're needed!

16

open the present!

We have different gifts, according to the grace given us.

Romans 12:6

THEME: **God's Gifts**

SCRIPTURE: *Romans 12:6–8; Matthew 25:14–30*

OPEN UP

(10–15 minutes)

1. If you could give *anything* to the person sitting on your left, what would you want to give? Describe it, and tell why you'd want to give it to that person.

Small Group Tip: *For Extra Fun*

If you can wrap up an empty box and bring it to small group, use that as an object of focus for question 1. Pass the wrapped box from person to person and ask group members to tell about the imaginary gifts they'd like to put in the box for each person.

OPEN BOOK

(15–25 minutes)

2. What do the gifts we receive tell us about the personality and priorities of the giver?

Have group members read Romans 12:6–8.

3. What do the gifts listed here tell us about God's personality and priorities?

4. Why do you suppose God has chosen to give each of us different gifts? Doesn't he expect the same things from all of us? Explain.

5. Paul's expectation is that God's gifts to us should continually be in use. Is that a realistic assumption for a twenty-first-century Christian in America? Defend your answer.

Backseat Bible: *Matthew 25:14–30*

The term "talent" used in this parable originally referred to a measure of weight (about seventy-five pounds), but by Jesus's time it was a system for counting money.[3] A talent was a huge sum—equal to about ten thousand denarii. If you consider that one denarius was average for a day's pay, then the servant who received the least still had over twenty-seven years worth of wages to invest! As such, this parable illustrates not only our stewardship responsibility, but also the nearly incomprehensible wealth of our master.[4]

Today the term "talent" no longer refers to money but has evolved to mean a gift or ability inherent in a person—a definition whose origin can be traced directly back to Jesus's parable of the talents in Matthew 25:14–30.[5]

Have group members read Matthew 25:14–30.

6. At first look, what does this parable say to you?

7. Although at least one servant was able to hide his master's endowment, none of the servants was able to decline

the master's money, or even to ask for a different gift. Do you think that's significant? Why or why not?

8. Are God's gifts to us always "investments," or something else? Explain.

OPEN LIFE **OPEN LIFE** (5–10 minutes)

9. How does our relationship with the Giver affect our ability to multiply the gifts God has given us?

10. What can you give to the person on your left to help him or her multiply God's gifts this week?

Small Group Tip

Encourage group members to be specific in the way they answer "Open Life" questions. Also, instruct people to wait a minute or two in silence before answering. This will give them an opportunity to think through their responses a bit before having to talk.

17

never give up

The LORD is good to those whose hope is in him.

Lamentations 3:25

THEME: **Hope**

SCRIPTURE: *Lamentations 3:21–26;*
Psalm 27:13–14

OPEN UP

(10–15 minutes)

1. Cup your hands in front of you and close your eyes. Imagine that when you open your eyes, something that you are really hoping for will miraculously appear in your open palms. What do you want to see there? Describe it.

OPEN BOOK

(15–25 minutes)

2. What makes it difficult for you to maintain hope in life? Explain.

Have group members read Lamentations 3:21–26.

3. Jeremiah wrote these words after being made a prisoner of war in Babylon. What emotions do you think he felt while he wrote this?

4. How do you think Jeremiah's memories of God in the past influenced his hope for the future?

5. What kinds of memories from your past help you to have hope for your future?

Backseat Bible: *Lamentations 3:21–26*

Because of the language and imagery used here, some theologians believe that Jeremiah wrote this as he was remembering the account of God's appearance to Moses recorded in Exodus 34. It was then that God replaced the tablets containing the Ten Commandments and made a covenant of prosperity and victory with Moses—and by extension, with the people of Israel.[6]

Have group members read Psalm 27:13–14.

6. King David wrote this song during a time when enemies surrounded him.[7] What part of his lyrics in Psalm 27:13–14 jump out and grab your attention?

7. What makes it difficult for you to believe the hopeful promise of Psalm 27:13–14? What makes it easy?

8. What part does waiting play in hope? And what do you think God expects us to do while we wait for his goodness to be seen?

OPEN LIFE (5–10 minutes)

9. What can you learn from Jeremiah and King David to help fuel your hope in God today?

10. Close your eyes, cup your hands in front of you, and think of the week ahead. Imagine that when you open your eyes, something that reflects the hope of Lamentations

3:21–26 and Psalm 27:13–14 will miraculously appear in your palms to help you this week. What do you think you'll see?

Small Group Tip

Encourage group members to be specific in the way they answer "Open Life" questions. Also, instruct people to wait a minute or two in silence before answering. This will give them an opportunity to think through their responses a bit before having to talk.

18

better than circumstance

Shout for joy to the LORD, all the earth.

Psalm 100:1

THEME: **Joy**

SCRIPTURE: *1 Thessalonians 5:16; Psalm 100*

OPEN UP

(10–15 minutes)

1. Cover your face with your hands. When I count to three, uncover your face and make an expression that demonstrates pure joy. Ready? 1–2–3! Looking at all these faces right now, what thoughts about joy come to your mind?

Small Group Tip: *For Extra Fun*

If your small group is the artistic sort, and if you have the time and access to art supplies, have people take a few minutes to create "Masks of Joy" for their responses to question 1. Then have people hold their masks in front of their faces and talk about interesting thoughts the masks bring to mind.

OPEN BOOK

(15–25 minutes)

2. "Joy is essentially a religious experience."[8] Do you agree or disagree with this statement? Defend both sides.

Have group members read 1 Thessalonians 5:16.

3. This command is physically and emotionally impossible. So why would the apostle Paul—and God (as the ultimate author of Scripture)—make it?

4. Is it sinful to be depressed? Explain.

5. What does true joy, like that commanded in 1 Thessalonians 5:16, look like? What does it feel like? Sound like?

Backseat Bible: *1 Thessalonians 5:16*

Is joy something that comes from within a person regardless of his or her outward circumstances, or is it something that wells up inside a person as a response to outside stimuli? The answer to that either/or question appears to be . . . *yes.*

When Paul wrote the command "be joyful always" in 1 Thessalonians 5:16, the Greek word he used for "joyful" was *chairete* (from the root *chairō*).[9] According to scholars, this word refers to *both* the inner "subjective state of joy" and outward, circumstantial "things that bring joy."[10]

Have group members read Psalm 100.

6. Psalm 100 revels in God's presence and goodness with uninhibited joy. What keeps us from doing the same in our everyday lives?

7. In what ways is joy an effortless, natural response to God? In what ways does joy require effort?

8. What part does gratefulness play in a joyful lifestyle?

OPEN LIFE

(5–10 minutes)

9. What kind of legacy would you leave if joy were always evident in your life? Who would most feel the impact of that legacy?

10. How will you make time to experience joy this week? Be specific, and share your plans.

Small Group Tip

Consider the option of having group members share their "Open Life" answers with a partner instead of with the whole group. This might be especially helpful if yours is a newly formed small group.

Afterward, have partners pray together in pairs to close the session.

19

God's economy

Love of money is a root of all kinds of evil.

1 Timothy 6:10

THEME: **Money**

SCRIPTURE: *1 Timothy 6:6–11, 17–19*

OPEN UP

(10–15 minutes)

1. If you were given a million dollars and instructed to spend it entirely within the next twenty-four hours, what would you buy?

OPEN BOOK

(15–25 minutes)

2. Is it a sin to be rich? Defend your answer.

Have group members read 1 Timothy 6:6–11.

3. What do you think is the main message of 1 Timothy 6:6–11? Summarize it with a brand-new ad slogan that could be used on a billboard or TV commercial.

4. In this section of his letter to Timothy, Paul adapted and quoted a few common sayings about money from the philosopher Cicero and other extrabiblical sources.[11] Should those quotes still be considered God's Word on the topic of money? Why or why not?

5. How does one pursue "godliness with contentment" (v. 6)? And what is included in the "great gain" that results from it?

Backseat Bible: *1 Timothy 6:9*

It may surprise some to discover that, in the society where Paul wrote 1 Timothy, the standards for being considered "rich" were much different than they are today. In fact, the wealthy lifestyle (and accompanying temptations) that Paul referred to in 1 Timothy 6:9 is comparable to that of a middle-class American in the twenty-first century.

In other words, by Paul's standards, the majority of Christians in America today are already "rich"![12]

Have group members read 1 Timothy 6:17–19.

6. What commands for twenty-first-century Americans do you hear in this Scripture?

7. Who benefits when money is viewed—and used—in accordance with the principles of 1 Timothy 6:17–19? Be specific, and tell how that works.

8. First Timothy 6:18 advises those with money to: (a) do good, (b) be rich in good deeds, (c) be generous, and (d) be willing to share. How might those actions show up in a checkbook or debit card register?

OPEN LIFE ⬅

(5–10 minutes)

9. Imagine a scale where "root of evil" is a 1 and "tool for good deeds" is a 10. On that scale of 1 to 10, where does money rank in your life? Explain.

10. As you look ahead to next week, what would be a wise prayer focus for you regarding the topic of money?

Small Group Tip

Encourage group members to be specific in the way they answer "Open Life" questions. Also, instruct people to wait a minute or two in silence before answering. This will give them an opportunity to think through their responses a bit before having to talk.

20

perfect peace

Do what leads to peace.

Romans 14:19

THEME: **Peace**

SCRIPTURE: *John 14:27; Romans 14:19*

OPEN UP ►

(10–15 minutes)

1. Where do you feel most peaceful? Describe that place and tell why it makes you feel at peace.

Small Group Tip: *For Extra Fun*

If there's a travel agency nearby, and if you have time ahead of your meeting, consider collecting a few travel brochures to bring to your small group. Then, for question 1, pass out the brochures and ask group members to tell which locations they think would provide the most peaceful vacations.

Small Group Tip

Because of America's involvement in recent wars, the topic of peace has potential to become politically charged. If some in your small group see this discussion as an opportunity to launch into political harangues, gently remind everyone that the purpose here is neither to shape public policies nor to pass judgment on political parties. Rather, the focus is to explore more deeply what it means to *personally* experience—and spread—Christ's peace in everyday life.

OPEN BOOK

(15–25 minutes)

2. What makes it difficult for you to experience peace today?

Have group members read John 14:27.

3. Jesus promised to leave us his peace. What does that actually mean?

4. Christians today are involved in wars all across the globe. Plus, Christians often can't even get along with each other. How does that fit with Jesus's promise of peace?

5. How do we access Christ's peace in our personal lives? In our relationships? In a society that often acts hostile toward Christians?

Backseat Bible: *John 14:27*

In Scripture, "peace" is mentioned close to three hundred times and is *always* associated with God's presence. Additionally, it generally refers to much more than simply an absence of conflict. Drawing from both Hebrew and Greek terminology, the concept of peace in the Bible encompasses elements of well-being, wholeness, prosperity, safety, rest, no war, orderliness, tranquility, personal contentment, and spiritual restoration.[13]

Have group members read Romans 14:19.

6. What does peace look like at home? At work? At church? In our community?

7. What kinds of individual efforts lead to peace and mutual edification in those places?

8. What is our responsibility in promoting peace? What is God's?

OPEN LIFE

(5–10 minutes)

9. When have you experienced the supernatural sense of Jesus's peace? What happened?

10. What can we do, as a group, to be agents of Jesus's peace this week?

21

wait for it

Those who wait for the LORD will gain new strength.

Isaiah 40:31 NASB

THEME: **Patience**

SCRIPTURE: *Isaiah 40:31; Ecclesiastes 7:8–9*

OPEN UP

(10–15 minutes)

1. What is the longest you've ever waited in line? What motivated you to keep waiting?

OPEN BOOK

(15–25 minutes)

2. What's the longest you've ever waited on God to answer a prayer? What motivates you to keep waiting for answers from God?

Have group members read Isaiah 40:31.

3. The New American Standard Bible translates the first part of Isaiah 40:31 as, "Those who *wait* for the Lord." The New International Version renders it, "Those who *hope* in the Lord." Both translations are accurate, but which do you think better communicates the message of this passage? Why?

4. What part does hope play in patience? How does that work when it comes to prayer?

5. Isaiah 40:31 infers that the practice of patience can be both physically and emotionally exhausting. How does hoping in the Lord renew a person's physical and emotional strength?

Backseat Bible: *Isaiah 40:31*

To the ancient Hebrew, the imagery of an eagle in Isaiah 40:31 would have resonated with layers of meaning. In that culture, the eagle was deeply admired for its strength, speed, power in flight, vitality, keen senses (particularly vision), and long life. But perhaps most importantly, the eagle was known for its intense, devoted care of its children.[14]

Have group members read Ecclesiastes 7:8–9.

6. Ecclesiastes 7:8–9 mentions that "patience is better than pride." But what does pride have to do with patience? Explain.

7. When do you feel impatient or angry with God? What do you do about it?

8. When are you most likely to feel impatient and angry in your daily life? What might be helpful to you in those situations?

OPEN LIFE

(5–10 minutes)

9. Imagine we work at A+ Fortune Cookie Factory. Our job is to create ten or twenty "fortunes" with wise advice on

the topic of patience. What pithy sayings will we put in our cookies today?

10. Which wise saying can you take home to help you best remember to live out the promises of Isaiah 40:31 and Ecclesiastes 7:8–9 this week?

Small Group Tip

For questions 9 and 10, consider having group members work together in pairs or trios to come up with a few pithy sayings to share with the larger group. Also, if paper and pencils are available, it might be fun to use fortune cookie–sized slips of paper to record people's ideas.

22

pride of life

Pride goes before destruction.

Proverbs 16:18

THEME: **Pride**

SCRIPTURE: *Proverbs 16:18–19; Luke 18:9–14*

OPEN UP

(10–15 minutes)

1. It's mascot time! Our first task today is to pick an animal mascot that best represents the word "pride" and one that best represents "humility." What ideas do you have? Explain.

Small Group Tip: *For Extra Fun*

Sure, this little add-on idea probably won't work for every small group (especially if your group is mostly over forty!), but if your group has youthful energy or is filled with sports fans you might want to try it.

Get a few face-painting kits and share them with everyone. Have people work in teams of two to four. Each team is to decorate the face of one member to represent their best idea in response to the first question—and have fun!

(15–25 minutes)

2. What's the difference between bragging and humbly telling the truth?

Have group members read Proverbs 16:18–19.

3. When have you seen (or experienced) the truth of this Scripture played out in real life? What happened?

4. What is it about pride that causes such problems?

5. What makes humility healthy and low self-esteem unhealthy? How do we differentiate between the two?

Backseat Bible: *Luke 18:9–14*

Fast facts about Pharisees:

- In Jesus's day, Pharisees were among the most faithful followers of God.
- There were about six thousand Pharisees living at the time of Christ's ministry.
- Pharisees were dedicated to living an authentic, practical, holy lifestyle.
- Pharisees believed in a coming Messiah (but didn't believe that it was Jesus).
- Jesus's own actions and teaching occasionally reflected a Pharisaical influence (i.e., his religious observances, his teaching style, and even his teaching topics).
- A few Pharisees (like Nicodemus and Joseph of Arimathea) were actually welcomed as Jesus's disciples.[15]

Have group members read Luke 18:9–14.

6. What emotions do you have as you read this story of the Pharisee and the tax collector? Why do you think you feel that way?

7. How do you see principles from Proverbs 16:18–19 at work in this parable?

8. Why is it easy for us to see—and judge—the hubris of the Pharisee in this parable, but more difficult to see the arrogance that displays itself in our own daily lives?

OPEN LIFE

(5–10 minutes)

9. Don't answer this question out loud—just take a moment to think about it. If you were chosen to be the mascot for either pride or humility, which word would your lifestyle and attitude best represent?

10. Finish this sentence: "One way I can guard against foolish pride in my attitudes and actions this week is . . ."

Small Group Tip

Encourage group members to be specific in the way they answer "Open Life" questions. Also, instruct people to wait a minute or two in silence before answering. This will give them an opportunity to think through their responses a bit before having to talk.

23

do you see what God sees?

O LORD, open his eyes so he may see.

2 Kings 6:17

THEME: **Perspective**

SCRIPTURE: *2 Kings 6:8–23; Luke 19:1–10*

OPEN UP ▶

(10–15 minutes)

1. Press the tips of your thumb and forefinger together to form a circle. Close your left eye and hold the circle up to your right eye, then describe what you see. How did that simple action change your perspective on what's around you?

OPEN BOOK ▶

(15–25 minutes)

2. Which is more important, reality or the perception of reality? Defend both answers.

Have group members read 2 Kings 6:8–23.

3. What did the people in this Scripture "see"? What do you see in this Scripture?

4. How did truth change the intellectual perspective of the people involved? The emotional perspective? The physical perspective?

5. Both Elisha and his servant were followers of God—and in danger. Yet initially only one of them saw the situation from a true perspective. Why do you suppose God's true perspective is so often hidden from his followers?

Backseat Bible: *2 Kings 6:8–23*

Despite being enemies, the people of Aram—later known as Syria—were actually distant relatives of the Hebrews. Abraham, Jacob, and others in Israel's patriarchy came from Aramean lineage. One important legacy of that heritage was the Aramaic language. Portions of the Bible were written down in Aramaic, and it was the common language of the Jews in Israel (including Jesus and his disciples) during the time when Christ walked the earth.[16]

Have group members read Luke 19:1–10.

6. What issues of relational perception and perspective were at play when Zacchaeus met Jesus?

7. What tactics did Jesus use to overcome relational misperceptions in this situation? What tactics does he use to help us today?

8. What do you do when you know you have an incomplete perspective on life? What should you expect God to do in that situation?

OPEN LIFE

(5–10 minutes)

9. Often we must trust God even though he rarely shows us the whole truth of our situations. What makes that easier or harder for you?

10. What difference will today's discussion make in the way you view your circumstances this week? Your relationships?

Small Group Tip

Encourage group members to be specific in the way they answer "Open Life" questions. Also, instruct people to wait a minute or two in silence before answering. This will give them an opportunity to think through their responses a bit before having to talk.

24

mirror images of Christ

By this all men will know that you are my disciples, if you love one another.

John 13:35

THEME: **Sharing Faith**

SCRIPTURE: *John 13:34–35; Romans 1:16–17*

OPEN UP
(10–15 minutes)

1. Look at the person on your left. If you had never met that person before, what would you know about him or her just by looking?

OPEN BOOK
(15–25 minutes)

2. What do people in our world know about Christians just by looking at us? How about people here in our community?

Have group members read John 13:34–35.

3. How does actively loving each other show the world that we belong to Christ?

4. Close your eyes and try to think in pictures. What does it look like for Christians to fulfill Jesus's command to love? Describe it, both as an ideal and as part of your personal experience.

5. Authentic love can't be manufactured or forced. So what do we do when we just don't feel like loving each other?

Backseat Bible: *John 13:35*

That the apostle John was the one to record Jesus's words in John 13:35 is both ironic and testimony to the transforming truth of Christ's statement there. After all, this temperamental "Son of Thunder" (Mark 3:17) once wanted to *destroy an entire village* because people living there didn't welcome Christ (Luke 9:52–56)!

Yet it is John whose Gospel most ardently reveals God's love for us (John 3:16) and who became known to history as the "apostle of love." Decades after Christ's death and resurrection, his first epistle to the churches still echoed his master's command: "Dear friends, let us love one another" (1 John 4:7).[17]

Have group members read Romans 1:16–17.

6. How does Romans 1:16–17 fit with Jesus's command in John 13:35?

7. Define "not ashamed." How is that different from being pushy, disrespectful, or overbearing?

8. What is God's responsibility when the gospel is shared? What is our responsibility?

OPEN LIFE

(5–10 minutes)

9. What makes it difficult for you to live out the messages of John 13:34–35 and Romans 1:16–17 in your daily life?

10. What will you do this week to overcome those difficulties?

Small Group Tip

Encourage group members to be specific in the way they answer "Open Life" questions. Also, instruct people to wait a minute or two in silence before answering. This will give them an opportunity to think through their responses a bit before having to talk.

25

bloom it!

He who began a good work in you will carry it on to completion.

Philippians 1:6

THEME: **Spiritual Growth**

SCRIPTURE: *Philippians 1:6, 9–11;
Galatians 5:22–23*

OPEN UP

(10–15 minutes)

1. If you could grow *anything* in a garden, what would you want to grow? Why?

Small Group Tip: *For Extra Fun*

If the weather is nice and your group is willing, hold this meeting in a large vegetable or flower garden that's open to the public. And, hey—bring along picnic supplies and make the most of the moment!

OPEN BOOK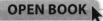

2. How does a person's spiritual growth mirror the way plants grow in a garden? Be specific in your comparison.

Have group members read Philippians 1:6, 9–11.

3. What do these verses tell you about spiritual growth? Do you see any comparisons to the way physical things grow?

4. What part does God play in bringing our spiritual growth to maturity? What part do we bring to the equation?

5. The fruit of righteousness comes through Jesus Christ (v. 11). What exactly does that mean, and how does that work when you're on the job? At home? Hanging out with friends?

Backseat Bible: *Galatians 5:22–23*

In the context of this passage, the Greek word for fruit (*karpos*)[18] refers to "a person's actions that result from his or her true character."[19] *Karpos* here is singular, indicating that *all* character qualities listed are present when the Holy Spirit is present in a life. Still, some theologians also suggest that the collection of character qualities here is divided into three overarching expressions of virtue: toward God (love, joy, peace); toward others (patience, kindness, goodness); toward oneself (faithfulness, gentleness, self-control).[20]

Have group members read Galatians 5:22–23.

6. How do you nurture the fruit of the Spirit in daily life?

7. Paul's message in Galatians 5:22–23 can be viewed as a *promise*, a *challenge*, and an *invitation*. Which of those words do you think is most accurate? Defend your answer.

8. It's tempting to use Galatians 5:22–23 as a measuring tool to judge the sincerity and/or authenticity of a person's Christian belief. What are the pros and cons of this kind of approach?

OPEN LIFE

(5–10 minutes)

9. If you could grow any character quality in yourself and see it come to fruition by the end of this week, what would you want to grow? Why?

10. What will you do to figuratively "plant a seed" toward this kind of growth in your life this week?

Small Group Tip

Encourage group members to be specific in the way they answer "Open Life" questions. Also, instruct people to wait a minute or two in silence before answering. This will give them an opportunity to think through their responses a bit before having to talk.

26

true is true

The truth will set you free.

John 8:32

THEME: **Truth**

SCRIPTURE: *John 8:31–41; 14:6*

OPEN UP

(10–15 minutes)

1. Make one statement about yourself that's true, and one that's not true—but don't tell the group which is which! Then everyone can answer this question: How can we best determine which statements are true?

OPEN BOOK

(15–25 minutes)

2. How do you determine what's true or false in your everyday life?

Have group members read John 8:31–41.

3. What does Jesus mean when he says "the truth will set you free"? How does that actually work?

4. Why do you suppose Jesus's audience reacted with hostility toward the truth that Jesus spoke?

5. When do you feel hostile toward truth? What do you do about it?

Backseat Bible: *John 8:41*

Although the full meaning is uncertain, some theologians suggest that the protests of the crowd recorded in John 8:41 were more than just theological debate.

When Jesus's audience said, "We are not illegitimate children," it could be interpreted as an insult directed at Christ, sarcastically insinuating that he himself was a bastard son— not the Son of God as he claimed. If that was actually the case, then in a moment of great irony, those people actually called the One who embodied eternal truth a liar.[21]

Have group members read John 14:6.

6. How does John 14:6 shed light on Jesus's comments in John 8:31–41?

7. If Jesus is THE truth, what does that mean exactly? Explain it as if you were speaking to a child.

8. Make one statement about Jesus that's true, and one that's false but widely accepted today. How are people supposed to determine which is actually the truth? How do Christians help or hinder people in discovering truth?

OPEN LIFE

(5–10 minutes)

9. When people reject Jesus's truth, or reject you because of God's truth, what's the best way to respond?

10. If you know Jesus, you know truth. How will that affect what you think and do this week?

Small Group Tip

For questions 9 and 10, consider having group members work together in pairs or trios to come up with a few ideas to share with the larger group.

discussion guides about family and community

27

kid connects

Let the little children come to me.

Mark 10:14

THEME: **Children**

SCRIPTURE: *Mark 10:13–16; Psalm 127:3–6*

OPEN UP (10–15 minutes)

1. What's your favorite memory from childhood? Describe it using all five senses (sight, smell, taste, touch, sound).

Small Group Tip: *For Extra Fun*

If you have time, and if group members are willing, have everyone bring a snack to share that somehow represents or is reminiscent of a favorite memory from childhood. (Mountain Dew and Funyuns optional!)

OPEN BOOK ↖

Have group members read Mark 10:13–16.

2. If you had been one of the children at this event, what do you imagine would have been your favorite memory born out of this moment? Describe it using the five senses.

3. What do Jesus's actions here tell you about him? About children?

4. When his best friends tried to protect him from being bothered by children, Jesus actually got angry about it (v. 14). Why do you suppose their good intentions ticked him off?

5. Parents wanted Jesus simply to lay a hand of blessing on their kids. Instead, he "took the children in his arms" to bless them (v. 16). What do you think that means? What might it have meant to the parents who were there? To the children he embraced?

6. How does it make you feel to know that Jesus expressly named a child to be your role model (vv. 14–15)?

Backseat Bible: *Mark 10:13–16*

The Greek word for children (*paidia*) that Mark used in verse 13 refers to anyone from infancy to age twelve. One unique aspect of this account is Mark's note that people wanted Jesus to *touch* their children (v. 13). Every other reference to Jesus touching people in Mark's Gospel indicates healing for the sick. But in Mark 10:13 alone it indicates "touching with the hands to impart blessing." Interestingly, Jesus imparted his blessing with more than simply a brush of the fingers: Jesus went overboard and "took the children in his arms" to bless them![1]

Have group members read Psalm 127:3–6.

7. In what ways are children a reward and a blessing for parents?

8. What about when our kids bring heartache and sorrow—in those situations when they definitely do *not* feel like a blessing? Does that kind of real life invalidate the message of Psalm 127:3–6? Defend your answer.

OPEN LIFE ➤

(5–10 minutes)

9. Based on our discussion today, what facts about children can we say are true?

10. How will these facts influence the way we act out—and experience—an intimate relationship with Jesus this week? Our relationships with others this week?

Small Group Tip

Encourage group members to be specific in the way they answer "Open Life" questions. Also, instruct people to wait a minute or two in silence before answering. This will give them an opportunity to think through their responses a bit before having to talk.

28

discipline dynamics

The LORD disciplines those he loves.

Proverbs 3:12

THEME: **Discipline**

SCRIPTURE: *Proverbs 3:11–12; Hebrews 12:5–11*

OPEN UP

(10–15 minutes)

1. The Discipline Committee called, and we're all in trouble for being too pretty and too smart! Fortunately, we get to choose our own punishments. So, would you rather: (a) get nine swats with a wooden paddle, (b) be grounded for the next month, (c) be forced to sit for twelve hours in a giant bowl of jelly, (d) stick your head in an aquarium filled with buzzing flies and keep it there for thirty minutes, or (e) change dirty diapers—left-handed—for an eight-hour shift? Explain your answer!

Small Group Tip: *For Extra Fun*

If yours is a talkative, uninhibited group, it might also be fun to ask group members to share the most unusual punishment they received as a child and/or the most unusual punishment they've given as an adult.

OPEN BOOK

(15–25 minutes)

2. How would you define the difference between discipline and punishment? Explain it as you would to a child.

Have group members read Proverbs 3:11–12.

3. In what ways does God, our heavenly Father, discipline us? How do we know the difference between God's discipline and God's punishment?

4. God disciplines because he loves. How does healthy discipline reveal true love? What does unwillingness to discipline reveal?

5. What parenting principles do you see from God's example as it's described in Proverbs 3:11–12? List them.

Backseat Bible: *Proverbs 3:12*

How many times does the book of Proverbs compare God to a father? Only once—right here in Proverbs 3:12. And in this context, it's a radical departure from traditional Old Testament thought. Jewish culture at this time generally regarded suffering as God's punishment for sin (see the book of Job). But Proverbs 3:12 reveals a counterintuitive truth: Sometimes our suffering is actually an expression of our heavenly Father's love for us—an act of correction designed for our ultimate good.[2]

Have group members read Hebrews 12:5–11.

6. Why is an intimate family relationship so important as the context for discipline? How does that play out in a relationship with God? In a parent's relationship with his or her own children?

7. The overarching purpose of God's correction is "our good" (v. 10). How does that translate into real life? Into the way we parent our own children?

8. What makes discipline difficult for you, both as a child of God and as the parent of a child? What's the healthiest response to those difficulties?

OPEN LIFE

(5–10 minutes)

9. If God is our heavenly Father, then he is both our role model and our mentor in parenting. What do you like best about God's parenting discipline in your life?

10. How can you imitate God in the way you parent your own children this week?

Small Group Tip

Encourage group members to be specific in the way they answer "Open Life" questions. Also, instruct people to wait a minute or two in silence before answering. This will give them an opportunity to think through their responses a bit before having to talk.

29

build up the body

Therefore encourage one another.

1 Thessalonians 5:11

THEME: **Encouraging Others**

SCRIPTURE: *Ephesians 4:29–32;*
1 Thessalonians 5:11

OPEN UP

(10–15 minutes)

1. If you had to speak in only TV or movie catchphrases, what quotable words could you use to encourage the person sitting closest to you? (You may have to explain why you chose your catchphrase!)

Small Group Tip

If people seem stumped by the catchphrase requirement of the first question, offer suggestions of fan-favorite, quotable movies like *Star Wars* and *Toy Story*, or TV shows like *The Office* or *Friends*. If group members are still stumped, rephrase

113

the question to use famous sayings instead (i.e., "Early to bed, early to rise, makes a man healthy, wealthy, and wise").

Also, for question 3, it may be worthwhile to have group members work together in pairs or trios to come up with a few ideas to share with the larger group. If paper and pencils are available, go ahead and have pairs/trios draw their targets and show them off to everyone!

OPEN BOOK

(15–25 minutes)

2. When was a time that encouraging words made a difference in your life? Tell about it.

Have group members read Ephesians 4:29–32.

3. If Paul's individual instructions in this passage were a circular target, what would be the bull's-eye and what would be in the rings surrounding that center? Explain your choices.

4. What does it take to speak "what is helpful for building others up according to their needs" (v. 29)? Be specific.

5. Think for a minute about verse 32. What pictures come to your mind that illustrate what Paul is talking about here?

Backseat Bible: *Ephesians 4:29*

The word Paul used for "unwholesome" in Ephesians 4:29 was often metaphorically associated with bad trees and rotten fruit. Thus, when Paul spoke of "unwholesome talk" that came out of a person's mouth, the mental image for his hearers was likely that of a diseased tree (representing a person) sprouting putrid fruit (corrupted words spoken through the mouth)![3]

Have group members read 1 Thessalonians 5:11.

6. Why did Paul feel it necessary to command the Thessalonians to do something ("encourage one another") that he knew they were already doing?

114

7. Why is it so important to encourage each other? Aren't we strong enough to do what's right on our own without needing constant encouragement from others?

8. How does the person receiving encouragement benefit from it? How does the person giving encouragement benefit?

OPEN LIFE

(5–10 minutes)

9. If God were here right now, sitting in a chair in this room, what kind of encouraging words do you think he'd say to us?

10. Ephesians 4:29–32 and 1 Thessalonians 5:11 are God's encouragement for us to encourage our families, friends, co-workers, pastors, and others. What are five ways we might do that individually this week? What's one way we can do that as a group this week?

Small Group Tip

Encourage group members to be specific in the way they answer "Open Life" questions. Also, instruct people to wait a minute or two in silence before answering. This will give them an opportunity to think through their responses a bit before having to talk.

30

bless 'em all (let God sort 'em out)

Seek the peace and prosperity of the city to which I have carried you.

Jeremiah 29:7

THEME: **Blessing Your Community**
SCRIPTURE: *Jeremiah 29:4–7; Luke 10:1–9*

OPEN UP ▸

(10–15 minutes)

1. Take a moment and silently brainstorm three strategies you could use to bless the person to your right—right now! (*Pause*) What ideas did you come up with?

Small Group Tip: *For Extra Fun*

If people are comfortable with it, have group members go ahead and act out some of their strategies for blessing each other in the group!

OPEN BOOK ▶

2. Why do you think it could be important to have a strategy for blessing others?

Have group members read Jeremiah 29:4–7.

3. What "city blessing" strategies do you see in this Scripture? How might they be applied to our local community?

4. What kind of personal or family commitment does it take to bless a city in this way? Describe it in terms of resources such as time, talent, finances, emotions, relationships, politics, structure, organization, faith, and so on.

5. In what ways is our church a blessing to our community? What keeps us from being more of a blessing?

Have group members read Luke 10:1–9.

6. What's your first reaction to Jesus's instructions here? What would you have asked him if you'd been there when he gave these directions?

7. This passage suggests that blessing a city involves both contentment (v. 8) and significance (v. 9). In what ways might serving our community bring out those qualities in the life of our church?

8. Why do you suppose Jesus wanted his disciples to go out and bless towns he intended to visit? And what implications might that have for us today?

Backseat Bible: *Luke 10:1–9*

It's important to note that when Jesus sent seventy-two of his followers out to bless the towns he intended to visit, he knew that people would oppose their work (v. 3). In fact, just days prior, he and his followers had actually been kicked out of a village by hostile Samaritans (Luke 9:51–56). In spite of the expected opposition, Jesus still sent his disciples—relatively unprotected—out to bless others on their way.

117

OPEN LIFE

9. If you knew you'd never be recognized or rewarded for it, what would realistically be enough to keep you committed to continually blessing our community? Be honest!

10. Take a moment and silently brainstorm three strategies you could use for blessing our community this week. (*Pause*) What ideas did you come up with?

Small Group Tip

Encourage group members to be specific in the way they answer "Open Life" questions. Also, instruct people to wait a minute or two in silence before answering. This will give them an opportunity to think through their responses a bit before having to talk.

31

compassion counts

When the kindness and love of God our Savior appeared, he saved us.

Titus 3:4–5

THEME: **Kindness**

SCRIPTURE: *Luke 10:30–37; Titus 3:3–6*

OPEN UP

(10–15 minutes)

1. This question is timed! I'm going to start a sentence, and then let's see how many ways we can complete it before sixty seconds are up. Ready? Finish this statement: "It takes guts to . . ."

OPEN BOOK

(15–25 minutes)

2. Now let's do the same thing for this statement: "It takes guts to show compassion because . . ."

Have group members read Luke 10:30–37.

3. Why was it a gutsy thing for the Samaritan in this parable to act with kindness?

4. In what ways do you see the character of Jesus reflected in this story? What else do you see?

5. Every day we have an opportunity to be a Good Samaritan to someone. What can we do to screw that up? And what can we do to take full advantage of that opportunity?

6. Realistically, how does a person balance his or her limited emotional and physical resources with Christ's command for us to show kindness and compassion like the Good Samaritan?

Backseat Bible: *Luke 10:30–37*

Although the story of the Good Samaritan fits easily into the designation of a "parable," some have wondered at its roots. Unlike most of Jesus's other parables, Luke never indicates that this story is fictional, leading some to think Jesus may have told of a real-life, historical example that he adapted to make his point.[4]

Also, early church fathers commonly viewed this parable as an allegory Jesus told about himself. In that view, Jesus's incarnation is represented in the person of the Samaritan traveling a dangerous road; his redemptive work is represented by the rescue of the traveler; his church is represented by the inn; and his triumphant second coming is represented by the promised return of the Samaritan at the end of the story.[5]

Have group members read Titus 3:3–6.

7. How does God's generosity toward you influence the way you show kindness to others (family members, friends, strangers, co-workers, or people you'll never even meet)?

8. Who deserves kindness? How does that affect the way you live out a compassionate lifestyle?

OPEN LIFE

(5–10 minutes)

9. This question is timed—see how many ways you can complete it before sixty seconds are up. Silently finish this sentence: "Lord, last week you were kind to me in these ways . . ."

10. How will you funnel God's persistent kindness toward you into the lives of your family members, friends, and others?

Small Group Tip

Consider the option of having group members share their "Open Life" answers with a partner instead of with the whole group. This might be especially helpful if yours is a newly formed small group.

Afterward, have partners pray together in pairs to close the session.

32

love is a four-letter word

Love never fails.

1 Corinthians 13:8

THEME: **Love**

SCRIPTURE: *1 Corinthians 13:1–13; Romans 5:8*

OPEN UP

(10–15 minutes)

1. Which of the following classic ad slogans best describes "love" for you? (a) "Good to the last drop." (b) "It's the real thing." (c) "Just do it." (d) "Like a good neighbor." (e) "Can you hear me now?" Explain your choice.

Small Group Tip: *For Extra Fun*

If your group members seem to enjoy the discussion prompted by question 1, you might follow up by asking people to create brand-new slogans that could be used in an ad campaign for "love."

122

(15–25 minutes)

2. Is love an innate ability in people or something that must be learned? Defend both viewpoints (if you can).

Have group members read 1 Corinthians 13:1–13.

3. If you were charged with creating a "Love Olympics" based on 1 Corinthians 13, what sporting events would you include? Why?

4. From what you see in this passage, what part of love is a feeling and what part of love is a decision? Explain.

5. In what ways does Jesus exemplify the message of 1 Corinthians 13? Be specific.

Backseat Bible: *1 Corinthians 13*

Fast facts about the Greek words for love:

Eros

- This term refers to physical desire or sexual expressions of love. Interestingly, although Scripture is not silent on the topic of sex, *eros* is never used in the New Testament.

Philos

- *Philos* is used frequently in the Bible and refers to a reciprocal, brotherly love.

Agapē

- This is the term Paul used in 1 Corinthians 13 and the one that appears most often in the New Testament when love is being discussed.

- *Agapē*, as used in the New Testament, refers to the highest ideal of love. It's a selfless, sacrificial love that puts the interests of others first.

- *Agapē* also includes elements of the following in its definition: forgiveness, redemption, spontaneity, caring, and reaching out to those who are undeserving.

- Although used widely in the New Testament, *agapē* appears only rarely in Greek philosophy and writings. It appears to have been a unique descriptor used by Christians in response to Jesus's incarnation.[6]

Have group members read Romans 5:8.

6. What does this verse add to the definition of love described in 1 Corinthians 13? How does that make you feel?

7. If God had not shown his love, how would that affect the way we love?

8. God loved us when we didn't love him. But we're (obviously!) not God. So, in a practical, human sense, how can we experience—and show—love when the object of our love does not reciprocate?

OPEN LIFE   (5–10 minutes)

9. What's the most important thing you've discovered from today's discussion on love?

10. How will that affect the way you experience love this week?

Small Group Tip

Encourage group members to be specific in the way they answer "Open Life" questions. Also, instruct people to wait a minute or two in silence before answering. This will give them an opportunity to think through their responses a bit before having to talk.

33

moms and dads matter

Train a child in the way he should go.

Proverbs 22:6

THEME: **Parenting**

SCRIPTURE: *Deuteronomy 6:6–9; Proverbs 22:6*

OPEN UP

(10–15 minutes)

1. What's your most vivid memory of your parents from your childhood? Describe it.

Small Group Tip: *For Extra Fun*

If paper and pencils are available, have people answer the first question by drawing stick-figure representations of their memories to share with the group.

OPEN BOOK

2. What impact, if any, did your parents have on your spiritual formation and growth? What did they do right? What did they do wrong?

Have group members read Deuteronomy 6:6–9.

3. What stands out for you the most when you read this Scripture?

4. "Love the LORD your God" prefaces the family instructions in this passage (v. 5). What happens if we try to pass God's commands on to our children without first loving the Lord?

5. Some say that loving the Lord makes passing on his commands a natural expression in our family relationships. Others say loving the Lord makes this instruction an obligation we must strive toward in our families. If you had to choose a side, what would you say? Defend your answer.

Backseat Bible: *Deuteronomy 6:6–9*

For thousands of years, adherents of Judaism have taken the instructions of Deuteronomy 6:6–9 quite literally. For instance, every synagogue service is expected to open with a declaration of Deuteronomy 6:4–5 (often called the *Shema*), and it's required to be spoken twice a day by the faithful Jew. In addition, the *Shema*—along with a few other biblical commands—is frequently inscribed on doorposts, and even written out on small scrolls that are attached to the forehead and the left arm.[7]

Have group members read Proverbs 22:6.

6. What does this command look like when lived out in a family today? Make a list.

7. What responsibility does a church community have in fulfilling this command? What responsibility does a divorced or noncustodial parent have?

8. What makes it easy or difficult for you to talk with your kids about a relationship with God? What does that mean in light of the command in Proverbs 22:6?

OPEN LIFE

(5–10 minutes)

9. By the time your children are eighteen, what are the top three things you want them to know personally about God?

10. What's the best thing you can do this week to help lead your children in discovering one or more of those things?

Small Group Tip

Encourage group members to be specific in the way they answer "Open Life" questions. Also, instruct people to wait a minute or two in silence before answering. This will give them an opportunity to think through their responses a bit before having to talk.

34

personal top 10

Love the Lord your God.

Matthew 22:37

THEME: **Priorities**

SCRIPTURE: *Matthew 22:35–40;*
Colossians 1:18–19

OPEN UP

(10–15 minutes)

1. Open your purse or wallet and look inside. If you were being robbed and could keep only one item in your purse or wallet, what would it be? Why does that item matter to you more than anything else in there?

OPEN BOOK

(15–25 minutes)

2. When you get up each morning, how do you decide what will matter most to you that day?

Have group members read Matthew 22:35–40.

3. The question posed in this Scripture is all about priorities in life. Why is it important to clearly identify what's most important? How does that show itself in the way you live?

4. Jesus's answer here seems like such an obvious one. Why do you suppose the questioner thought it would be a test for Christ?

5. What makes the command to love the Lord and love your neighbor a daily "test" for us?

Backseat Bible: *Matthew 22:36*

Rabbis in Jesus's time continued an ongoing debate about which parts of God's law were "weighty" (such as laws about murder and idolatry) and which were "light" (such as how to tithe garden vegetables).[8] Thus, the question posed in Matthew 22:36 was not some random inquiry by a curious audience member. Rather, it appears to have been more like a political test (see verse 35) to find out where Jesus stood on issues of religious law and morality. Jesus's answer would have put him on one side or another in the debate.

Have group members read Colossians 1:18–19.

6. How does Colossians 1:18–19 help or hinder our understanding of Matthew 22:35–40?

7. If Christ truly is everything Colossians 1:18–19 says he is, then why is it so easy for Christians to let other priorities in life crowd out his influence?

8. How does a person go about making Jesus the highest priority in life—without becoming an overbearing jerk or an irrelevant parent/friend/co-worker?

OPEN LIFE

(5–10 minutes)

9. Open your Bible to one (or both) of the passages we've read today. If you could keep only one truth out of these verses to take home with you, what would it be? Why?

10. What's one way that truth will affect the way you pursue your priorities in life this week? Be specific—and be honest!

Small Group Tip

Encourage group members to be specific in the way they answer "Open Life" questions. Also, instruct people to wait a minute or two in silence before answering. This will give them an opportunity to think through their responses a bit before having to talk.

35

fight fair

Serve one another in love.

Galatians 5:13

THEME: **Resolving Conflict**
SCRIPTURE: *Acts 15:1–35; Galatians 5:13–15*

OPEN UP

(10–15 minutes)

1. Imagine the United Nations has declared that all future conflicts between nations will be resolved by a sporting contest. What sport do you think best lends itself to that type of purpose? Why?

OPEN BOOK

(15–25 minutes)

2. What strategies do you find to be most effective for resolving conflict when it occurs in your family?

Have group members read Acts 15:1–35.

3. What conflict resolution strategies do you see being demonstrated in this account of the early church?

4. Apparently the disagreement at the center of Acts 15 was an angry one, with heated opinions delivered forcefully by both sides (v. 2). How does it make you feel to discover that early church leaders sometimes couldn't get along? Explain.

5. Based on what you see in Acts 15, what would you say is the ultimate goal of conflict resolution? How does that play out at home? At church? At work?

Backseat Bible: *Acts 15*

The enduring, irrevocable impact of the Council of Jerusalem recorded in Acts 15 simply can't be underestimated. It was here, finally, that the question of whether or not Christianity would be simply a sect of Judaism was answered once and for all.

The evangelistic success that Paul and Barnabas experienced among non-Jews forced the church fathers to decide this basic question: *Must a person become a Jew in order to become a Christian?* After much discussion and practical interpretation of what they saw God doing in the lives of Gentiles, the answer that came back was a definitive "No."[9]

Have group members read Galatians 5:13–15.

6. How does Galatians 5:13–15 describe—or *not* describe—the way you experienced conflict last week? Explain.

7. Is conflict between Christians sinful? Defend your answer.

8. How do we know when to fight for something and when to walk away from the fight? And how does that play out in daily life, right here where we live?

OPEN LIFE ➤

(5–10 minutes)

9. If we were the only people in the world praying for the healthy resolution of conflicts in our families, our community, and our nation, what would be the best use of our prayer time?

10. How will you pursue that kind of prayer time this week?

Small Group Tip

Encourage group members to be specific in the way they answer "Open Life" questions. Also, instruct people to wait a minute or two in silence before answering. This will give them an opportunity to think through their responses a bit before having to talk.

36

R-E-S-P-E-C-T

Show proper respect to everyone.

1 Peter 2:17

THEME: **Respect**

SCRIPTURE: *1 Peter 2:13–17; Ephesians 6:1–6*

OPEN UP

(10–15 minutes)

1. If you were charged with showing respect for the person on your right—without speaking a word—what would you do? Demonstrate it now.

Small Group Tip: *For Extra Fun*

To encourage creativity and increase the challenge of question 1, you might consider adding a rule that states no one can use the same demonstration of respect that another person has already used. Likewise, for question 2, you could suggest that no one can use the same word definition twice—but that people can coin new words if they like!

(15–25 minutes)

2. What if you were charged with creating a definition for respect using only one word? What word would you choose— and why?

Have group members read 1 Peter 2:13–17.

3. How would you rewrite the main message of this passage for twenty-first-century Americans? How about for twenty-first-century Iranians?

4. At this time, Christians were the object of intense slander in the Roman world—accusations that would soon devolve into torture and execution (v. 15).[10] Was it naïve for Peter to recommend showing respect and "doing good" as a strategy for silencing persecution? Defend your answer.

5. What does "proper respect to everyone" (v. 17) look like? Describe it in pictures.

Backseat Bible: *1 Peter 2:17*

Commenting on 1 Peter 2:17, renowned pastor and theologian Charles Swindoll admits "we live in the uncomfortable, constant tension of Peter's seemingly impossible commands." But Pastor Swindoll also points out that the apostle himself lived that same uncomfortable tension. During the time Peter wrote this letter, "Christians were scattered and mistreated, imprisoned, and enslaved. They were rejected by family members, singled out by employers, and attacked by law enforcement officials who were supposed to protect them. Besides these instances of day-to-day trials, all of them—throughout the empire—were living under an emperor growing increasingly insane and anti-Christian: Nero." In spite of this, Peter's life-response was still the same: *Show proper respect to everyone.*[11]

Have group members read Ephesians 6:1–6.

6. What elements of "proper respect" do you see on display in the instructions of Ephesians 6:1–6?

7. Judging by this Scripture, respect seems to include both attitude and actions. Which is more important? Why?

8. What happens when someone—a parent, child, boss, pastor, government official, etc.—doesn't deserve respect? What's the appropriate response then?

OPEN LIFE

(5–10 minutes)

9. If you were to take the heart of our discussion today and post it in 140 characters or less on Twitter.com, what would you say?

10. If you were to take that 140-character Tweet to heart this week, what changes would that mean in your daily life?

Small Group Tip

For questions 9 and 10, consider having group members work together in pairs or trios to come up with a few ideas to share with the larger group.

37

how low can you go?

I have set you an example that you should do as I have done for you.

John 13:15

THEME: **Service**

SCRIPTURE: *John 13:1–17; Romans 12:10–17*

OPEN UP

(10–15 minutes)

1. Servants R Us just called, and you've been given a gift certificate for one full day of help from a professional servant! What tasks will you have that servant perform for you?

Small Group Tip

It's unlikely, but possible, that some in your group will see questions 1 and 2 as opportunities to make off-color jokes about the sex industry. If that happens, simply remind the group that Servants R Us is prohibited from tasks that are either illegal or immoral and encourage people to think in more family-friendly discussion terms instead.

OPEN BOOK

(15–25 minutes)

2. What if you worked for Servants R Us—what would people hire you to do?

Have group members read John 13:1–17.

3. What characteristics of an authentic servant lifestyle do you see in Jesus? List them.

4. Jesus washed the feet of Judas—knowing that Judas would later betray him. How does that make you feel? Explain.

5. "Sometimes the best act of service is to do nothing at all." Do you agree or disagree with that statement? Defend your view and share examples with your answer.

Backseat Bible: *John 13:6–10*

When Jesus came to wash his feet, Peter asked to have his head and hands washed as well, as a symbolic cleansing. Christ's response was that Peter had already "bathed" (Greek *louō*, a complete washing) and now needed only to have his feet "washed" (Greek *niptō*, a splash).

The word picture here, symbolic of Christ's cleansing from sin, is that of a person returning home from a public bathhouse. While the body (and head and hands) remained clean, the feet would need a light touch-up (a splash) at home to wash off the dust of the road.[12]

Have group members read Romans 12:10–17.

6. If Romans 12:10–17 were the job description used by Servants R Us, how easy or difficult would it be to get hired? Why?

7. How can a person pursue an authentic, servant lifestyle as it's described in this passage—without burning out or becoming overwhelmed? Be specific.

8. Who in your life has best exemplified Romans 12:10–17 for you? Describe that person and the impact of his or her example.

OPEN LIFE ▶

(5–10 minutes)

9. What's the most important thing you discovered about servanthood during our discussion today?

10. How will that affect the way you live a servant lifestyle tomorrow?

Small Group Tip

Encourage group members to be specific in the way they answer "Open Life" questions. Also, instruct people to wait a minute or two in silence before answering. This will give them an opportunity to think through their responses a bit before having to talk.

38

trust exercises

Don't be afraid; just believe.

Mark 5:36

THEME: **Trusting God**

SCRIPTURE: *Mark 5:21–24, 35–42; Proverbs 3:5–6*

OPEN UP

(10–15 minutes)

1. Stand up and look at your chair. Go ahead and give it a good inspection right now! What was it about that chair that prompted you to trust it so completely to hold your weight?

OPEN BOOK

(15–25 minutes)

2. How does trust work? What does it require?

Have group members read Mark 5:21–24, 35–42.

3. Jesus asked Jairus to trust him, despite the obviously poor circumstances. What emotions do you think Jairus experienced during this encounter with Christ? Start at their initial meeting and make a list that goes through to the end of the story.

4. How do emotions affect our ability to trust in God's promises?

5. Jesus encouraged Jairus to trust by saying, "Don't be afraid" (v. 36). Why do you suppose that was necessary? And what does that imply for us today?

6. If Jairus were here right now, what would you ask him? And how do you think he'd respond?

Backseat Bible: *Mark 5:35–42*

It's traditionally believed that Jairus's daughter actually died and was brought back to life by Jesus. Some theologians, however, are reluctant to accept that view because it discounts Christ's own announcement that the girl was "not dead but asleep" (see v. 39). They suggest that the child was, instead, suffering from an undiagnosed diabetic coma—something unknown at that time—and that Jesus miraculously resuscitated her, saving her from impending death. Jesus's command to "give her something to eat" (v. 43) also lends credence to this view.[13]

Have group members read Proverbs 3:5–6.

7. How was Jairus an example of this Scripture being lived out in Jesus's time? How does a person live out Proverbs 3:5–6 today?

8. How do we know when it's time to trust God for a miracle, and when we must trust God to help us endure *without* a miracle? Explain.

OPEN LIFE

(5–10 minutes)

9. What's one area of your life that requires you to trust God this week? Be specific.

10. With that in mind, what can we do to help each other remember Jesus's encouragement, "Don't be afraid; just believe"?

Small Group Tip

Encourage group members to be specific in the way they answer "Open Life" questions. Also, instruct people to wait a minute or two in silence before answering. This will give them an opportunity to think through their responses a bit before having to talk.

39

work it out

Serve wholeheartedly, as if you were serving the Lord.

Ephesians 6:7

THEME: **Work**

SCRIPTURE: *Ephesians 6:7–9; Titus 3:1–2, 8*

OPEN UP ⬈

(10–15 minutes)

1. Let's imagine you could get paid a million dollars a year to do whatever work you wanted to do. What would be your dream job? Consult with the person next to you to come up with a brief job description.

Small Group Tip

This discussion centers on practical expressions of Ephesians 6:7–9 and Titus 3:1–2, 8 in a work setting. However, some in your group may be currently unemployed, not employed outside the home, or seeking a new job. Feel free to adapt the questions here to include those people and their situations as appropriate.

OPEN BOOK ➤

(15–25 minutes)

2. What makes a job satisfying?

Have group members read Ephesians 6:7–9.

3. What does this passage tell you about finding satisfaction in your work?

4. Work is often unpleasant. Co-workers are often disagreeable and sometimes dishonest. Supervisors are often uncaring jerks or incompetent leaders. How are we supposed to fulfill Ephesians 6:7–9 in situations like that?

5. What does this Scripture mean for those of us who are supervisors at work?

Backseat Bible: *Ephesians 6:7–9*

It may seem morally awkward for Paul to address instructions to slaves and their masters in Ephesus without condemning the practice of slavery. It's important to remember, however, that at this time in the city of Ephesus slaves made up about one-third of the entire population and slavery was a harsh fact of life.

In light of that fact, Paul's declaration that both slave and master served one Lord—Jesus Christ—was a radical change of perspective with two significant implications: (1) Slaves gained dignity in serving an earthly master as though serving Christ, and (2) masters gained an obligation to treat slaves with the same dignity they would afford to Jesus.[14]

Have group members read Titus 3:1–2, 8.

6. What does this Scripture have to say about job performance for Christians?

7. Verse 1 tells us to "be ready to do whatever is good." Verse 8 reiterates that sentiment with instructions for us to devote ourselves "to doing what is good." Why repeat that message?

8. What part of the instructions in this passage are hardest for you personally? Why—and what can be done about it?

OPEN LIFE

(5–10 minutes)

9. Let's imagine you could get paid a million dollars a year for living out the instructions of Ephesians 6:7–9 and Titus 3:1–2, 8 in your current job. For you, what would it take to do that?

10. What have you learned from today's discussion that might help you "serve wholeheartedly, as if you were serving the Lord" in your work this week?

Small Group Tip

Encourage group members to be specific in the way they answer "Open Life" questions. Also, instruct people to wait a minute or two in silence before answering. This will give them an opportunity to think through their responses a bit before having to talk.

discussion guides about holidays

40

new year's day

The old life is gone; a new life has begun!

2 Corinthians 5:17 NLT

THEME: **New Beginnings**

SCRIPTURE: *2 Corinthians 5:17; John 3:1–8*

OPEN UP

(10–15 minutes)

1. The Future Zoo Project called, and they want us to create an all-new creature for display on January 1, 2050! What ideas can we come up with?

Small Group Tip: *For Extra Fun*

It might be fun to make the first question into a little contest for your small group. Have people work in pairs to come up with their most creative ideas, then present them to the group at large. Vote to see which is the favorite!

OPEN BOOK

2. What is it about a new year and new things that we find so attractive? Explain.

Have group members read 2 Corinthians 5:17.

3. What do you see that's attractive about the promise of newness in this Scripture?

4. Second Corinthians 5:17 speaks of more than just an upgrade or improvement over what currently exists. Instead, it promises an entirely new beginning. Exactly what does that mean for us?

5. How did your new beginning in Christ come about?

Small Group Tip

Question 5 is an opportunity for people to remember—and share—about how they first became a Christian. For some this will be easy and enjoyable. For others it may feel a little uncomfortable. And for those who are not yet Christians, it could be irrelevant.

Be sensitive to your group members and their spiritual progress at this point. If people feel uncomfortable, a way to lighten the pressure could be to begin by first telling how you became a Christian and then asking if anyone has a similar story they'd like to share.

Backseat Bible: *John 3:4*

Although Nicodemus appeared to be surprised by Jesus's assertion that new birth was required for salvation (v. 4), the idea was not new.

According to theologian Craig S. Keener, Jewish teachers at this time often referred to people who converted to Judaism as "starting life anew like 'newborn children.'" As a Pharisee and a member of the Jewish ruling council, Nicodemus should have understood immediately that Jesus wasn't talking about physical rebirth (see John 3:7), but he didn't. Go figure.[1]

Have group members read John 3:1–8.

6. What's your first impression of Nicodemus? Why do you suppose he came to Jesus?

7. Jesus's comments in verse 3 seem to have nothing to do with Nicodemus's introductory statement in verse 2—yet Scripture indicates they were spoken "in reply." What do you think was really going on?

8. "You must be born again" (v. 7). What parts of that new beginning can be seen in a person's life? What can't be seen?

OPEN LIFE

(5–10 minutes)

9. The Future You Project called, and they want to know what kind of new beginning you need most from Jesus right now. What will you tell them?

10. What kind of prayer will help you find that new beginning this week?

Small Group Tip

Consider the option of having group members contemplate their "Open Life" answers individually or with a partner instead of with the whole group. This might be especially helpful if yours is a newly formed small group.

Also, some in your group may see questions 9 and 10 as an opportunity to begin a new relationship with Jesus by becoming a Christian. Be open and prepared to lead someone through that life-changing experience if the opportunity presents itself.

41

groundhog day

He guides me in paths of righteousness.

Psalm 23:3

THEME: **God's Guidance**

SCRIPTURE: *Psalm 23; John 16:13–15*

OPEN UP
(10–15 minutes)

1. This February 2, the venerable groundhog is going into retirement! Who or what would you nominate to take the groundhog's place in guiding our preparations for spring? Defend your nomination.

OPEN BOOK
(15–25 minutes)

2. Why do we like little traditions like Groundhog Day to help guide us in our daily lives? What does that say about the inherent needs of people?

Have group members read Psalm 23.

3. How does it make you feel to think of the Lord as a shepherd and a guide in life? Explain.

4. In what ways have you seen God be a shepherd who leads you? What happened?

5. If we were honest, we'd admit that sometimes when we try to follow God's leading, we end up in places that don't match the imagery of Psalm 23. So what happened?

Backseat Bible: *Psalm 23:4*

The psalmist's image of God as a shepherd who "guides . . . in paths of righteousness" (v. 4) includes layered richness inherent in its meaning.

First, it indicates that God takes us on "right tracks" that lead *somewhere*—to a specific destination. God doesn't lead aimlessly, or force us simply to wander and backtrack to use up time. Second, God leads to abundant provision for our present needs, symbolized by the physical needs of a sheep: pasture (food), rest (safety, shelter), and water.[2] Third, the context and wording here denote "to lead into Paradise"—indicating that God ultimately will lead us safely into heaven.[3]

Have group members read John 16:13–15.

6. Like the promise of Psalm 23, Christ promised that the Holy Spirit would actively guide us through life. How does that happen?

7. If history has taught us anything, it's that the Holy Spirit sometimes leads Christians into difficult—even deadly—circumstances. How does that harmonize with what we've read in Scripture today?

8. Sometimes, when we seek God's guidance, the Holy Spirit seems silent. What's the best thing to do then?

OPEN LIFE

(5–10 minutes)

9. If Jesus physically came to your home and spent one day with you, how might his leading change what happens in your life? In your home? At your work? When you are alone?

10. How will you invite Jesus to lead you each day this week?

Small Group Tip

Encourage group members to be specific in the way they answer "Open Life" questions. Also, instruct people to wait a minute or two in silence before answering. This will give them an opportunity to think through their responses a bit before having to talk.

42

super bowl sunday

He gives us the victory through our Lord Jesus Christ.

1 Corinthians 15:57

THEME: **Victory**

SCRIPTURE: *1 Corinthians 9:16–27; 15:51–58*

OPEN UP

(10–15 minutes)

1. Who do you think will be victorious in the Super Bowl this year? Make a prediction—complete with final score!

Small Group Tip: *For Extra Fun*

Hey, here's an unexpected idea: Why not hold this small group meeting in the afternoon before the big game on Super Bowl Sunday? (Go Cleveland Browns!)

Also, this discussion guide (combined with a Super Bowl party) is a good way to launch a brand-new small group—so feel free to use it that way!

(15–25 minutes)

2. What kind of training and dedication do you think it takes to achieve victory in the Super Bowl? Sum it up in five principles that could be shared with aspiring athletes.

Have group members read 1 Corinthians 9:16–27.

3. Based on what you see in this passage, what kind of training and dedication do you think it takes to achieve daily victory in the Christian life? Sum it up in five principles for followers of Jesus.

4. What are some of the rewards of dedicated training for victory in the Christian life? Be specific, and make a list.

5. In what ways is God like a coach for those who desire to follow Christ? How does he prepare and empower us to live faithfully for Jesus?

Backseat Bible: *1 Corinthians 9:24–27*

The athletic metaphor for Christian living would have been immediately recognized by Paul's Corinthian readers. Living in that major city, they would have been very familiar with the Greek Olympic Games, as well as with local athletes involved in the Isthmian Games.

Additionally, Paul's reference to being "disqualified" (v. 27) would have brought to mind the image of an official herald at Greek sporting events. It was the herald's job to announce to the crowd the names of any contestants who had been deemed unworthy to compete.[4]

Have group members read 1 Corinthians 15:51–58.

6. What emotions do you feel when you read about this victory we have in Christ? Why do you feel that way?

7. How do we experience firsthand the kind of victory in Christ that's talked about here? Describe it.

OPEN LIFE

(5–10 minutes)

8. What obstacles seem to interfere with your Christian training and daily victory in Christ?

9. This week, what can you do to overcome those obstacles? Who can help you in that effort?

Small Group Tip

Consider the option of having group members share their "Open Life" answers with a partner instead of with the whole group. This might be especially helpful if yours is a newly formed small group.

Afterward, have partners pray together in pairs to close the session.

43

valentine's day

Submit to one another out of reverence for Christ.

Ephesians 5:21

THEME: **Marriage**

SCRIPTURE: *Ephesians 5:21–33;*
1 Corinthians 7:1–5

OPEN UP

(10–15 minutes)

1. What's the best love story you've ever read or seen as a movie? What made it so great for you?

Small Group Tip: *For Extra Fun*

This small group meeting is fun to do as part of a couples' dinner party or Valentine's Day get-together!

OPEN BOOK

2. There are millions of books about love and marriage. Why do you suppose that this topic has been so popular throughout history and across cultures?

Have group members read Ephesians 5:21–33.

3. If you were writing a book about marriage that was based on Ephesians 5:21–33 and intended for couples in our community, what would some of the chapter titles be? Describe them and tell a little about the content of the chapters as well.

4. "Submit to one another out of reverence for Christ" (v. 21). What does that mean in daily, practical terms? Explain it and give examples if you can.

5. Some say that the instructions about marriage in Ephesians 5:21–33 are designed to make women subservient to men. What are your thoughts on that? Defend your views.

Backseat Bible: *1 Corinthians 7:5*

During Paul's day, some taught that sexual intercourse in marriage was an unholy necessity that was fraught with impurity. In their view, true righteousness meant abstaining from sex completely, even between husbands and wives—or at least having sex as infrequently as possible (for instance, only to have children) so as to minimize the associative impurity.[5]

Paul's clearheaded debunking of that myth—and straightforward instruction for married couples to make sexual activity a regular habit—was probably surprising to some of his contemporaries. At the same time, it also reaffirmed God's holy blessing on sex as part of a healthy marriage relationship.

Have group members read 1 Corinthians 7:1–5.

6. Is the apostle Paul—a person admittedly opposed to marriage—actually giving sex advice to couples here? What gives him the right to do that?

7. What do you see that might be surprising or unexpected about Paul's sex advice here? Explain.

8. What do you see that's wise about Paul's sex advice? Explain.

OPEN LIFE

(5–10 minutes)

9. How can the guidelines outlined in Ephesians 5:21–33 and 1 Corinthians 7:1–5 contribute to your real-life love story?

10. What can you do this week to begin writing your love story like that?

Small Group Tip

Encourage group members to be specific in the way they answer "Open Life" questions. Also, instruct people to wait a minute or two in silence before answering. This will give them an opportunity to think through their responses a bit before having to talk.

44

st. patrick's day

There was a disciple named Tabitha . . . who was always doing good.

Acts 9:36

THEME: **Legacies**

SCRIPTURE: *2 Timothy 4:14–15; Acts 9:36–43*

OPEN UP

(10–15 minutes)

1. What's the most interesting bit of trivia you know about St. Patrick's Day?

Small Group Tip: *For Extra Fun*

If your small group is the competitive sort, form two teams and use the trivia questions below for a little St. Patrick's Day trivia contest![6] The team with the most correct answers wins.

1. True or false: St. Patrick was Irish. *(False. He was actually British.)*

2. St. Patrick first came to Ireland as: (a) a tourist visiting his family; (b) a slave who was kidnapped from his home in England; (c) a missionary sent by the Catholic Church. *(Answer: b. He was kidnapped as a boy and spent six years as a slave in Ireland before he finally escaped.)*

3. True or false: St. Patrick's real name was Patrick. *(False. His birth name is unknown, though many think it was probably Maewyn.)*

4. We celebrate St. Patrick's Day on March 17 because: (a) that was the date he returned to Ireland as a Catholic missionary; (b) that was his birthday in AD 380; (c) that was the day he died in AD 461. *(Answer: c. That was the day he died.)*

5. We associate the shamrock with St. Patrick because: (a) it's the national flower of Ireland; (b) St. Patrick loved shamrock stew and shared it with the poor; (c) St. Patrick used the shamrock to explain the Trinity (Father, Son, Holy Spirit). *(Answer: c. Once, while preaching on the Trinity, he picked a shamrock and used it to illustrate his point. The rest is history!)*

OPEN BOOK

(15–25 minutes)

2. What does the story of St. Patrick tell us about one person's ability to leave a lasting legacy? And why is that important?

Have group members read 2 Timothy 4:14–15.

3. How would you compare the legacy left by Alexander the metalworker to the legacy left by St. Patrick?

4. Alexander's hurtful actions have been remembered and preserved for thousands of years. How do you think he would feel if he knew about that? Explain.

5. What influence would it have if you knew that your attitudes and actions would be remembered and talked about in small group studies for the next two thousand years?

162

Backseat Bible: *2 Timothy 4:14*

Alexander the metalworker is not mentioned anywhere else in Scripture—although some theologians speculate that he might have been the same person referenced as a false teacher in 1 Timothy 1:19–20.[7] Others suspect that, because of his hostility toward Paul's preaching about Christ, he was an informant who helped the authorities arrest Paul and trump up charges against him.[8]

Have group members read Acts 9:36–43.

6. What's your first impression of Tabitha (Dorcas) and the life she lived? Describe it.

7. Tabitha is introduced here as a "disciple." Does that surprise you? Why or why not?

8. What does Tabitha's example tell us about leaving a lasting legacy as one of Christ's disciples?

OPEN LIFE

(5–10 minutes)

9. If they were to replace St. Patrick's Day with a holiday about your life, what would you want people to celebrate?

10. This week, what's one thing we can learn from St. Patrick, Alexander the metalworker, and Tabitha to help us plant good seeds for a lasting legacy?

Small Group Tip

For questions 9 and 10, consider having group members work together in pairs or trios to come up with a few ideas to share with the larger group.

45

easter

He has risen!

Mark 16:6

THEME: **Jesus's Resurrection**

SCRIPTURE: *Mark 16:1–11; 1 Corinthians 15:1–20*

OPEN UP

(10–15 minutes)

1. What's one thing about you that others here would be surprised to discover? Take a second to think about it, and then share it with the rest of us.

Small Group Tip: *For Extra Fun*

If time and resources permit, consider turning this small group into a "surprise party" of sorts. Begin your meeting with traditional trappings like balloons, confetti, banners, and the ubiquitous shout of "Surprise!" Then serve cake and punch to go along with your discussion time.

OPEN BOOK ▶

2. What's required for something to truly be a surprise? Make a list of regulations that the "Surprise Police" could use.

Have group members read Mark 16:1–11.

3. From what you see in this passage, how well does Jesus's resurrection comply with the regulations of our Surprise Police?

4. In Mark's Gospel alone, Jesus predicted his resurrection three times (see Mark 8:31; 9:31; and 10:34). So why was it surprising to find Jesus's tomb empty?

5. What emotions do you think the women at Jesus's tomb felt when they discovered it was empty? How does that compare to the way you feel today when you think about Jesus's resurrection?

Backseat Bible: *Mark 16:1–11*

One of the many surprises surrounding the historical record of Jesus's resurrection is the fact that women were the first to discover—and testify about—Christ's return from the dead.

Under Jewish law at that time, women were barred from being witnesses in court, and a woman's testimony was routinely discounted simply because it came from a woman. (Even Jesus's disciples initially disbelieved Mary's account of Jesus's resurrection—see verse 11.) Yet the Gospel of Mark unapologetically records the role women played in witnessing Jesus's return to life. That suggests two things: (1) Mark's account is historically accurate (otherwise a more culturally authoritative "witness" would have been chosen), and (2) women are important to Jesus![9]

Have group members read 1 Corinthians 15:1–20.

6. This single event—Jesus's resurrection—has never been completely explained away, despite many attempts throughout

history. Why is it such a big deal whether or not it really happened?

7. The world's major religions generally acknowledge that Jesus lived, that he was a good man, and that he was crucified. Yet only Christians believe he was raised from the dead and continues to live today. Are we just deceiving ourselves? Defend your answer.

8. What kind of personal experience have you had with the risen Christ? Describe one specific encounter.

 OPEN LIFE

(5–10 minutes)

9. "Christ has indeed been raised from the dead" (1 Cor. 15:20). What implications does that statement have for you right now?

10. This week, what can we do to help each other encounter anew our risen Christ?

Small Group Tip

Encourage group members to be specific in the way they answer "Open Life" questions. Also, instruct people to wait a minute or two in silence before answering. This will give them an opportunity to think through their responses a bit before having to talk.

46

mother's day

If anything is excellent or praiseworthy—think about such things.

Philippians 4:8

THEME: **Motherhood**

SCRIPTURE: **Ephesians 6:2–3; Philippians 4:8–9**

OPEN UP

(10–15 minutes)

1. We've been put in charge of the president's new "Moms Rock!" celebration on the White House lawn. What fun stuff should we do to honor mothers at this nationally televised event?

OPEN BOOK

(15–25 minutes)

2. The idea of honoring your mother is rooted in the Ten Commandments in the Bible—yet no one protests for a

"separation of church and state" on this issue. Why do you suppose that is?

Have group members read Ephesians 6:2–3.

3. On a personal level, does the command of Ephesians 6:2 feel more like a *privilege* or a *chore* for you? Explain.

4. Some think the promise in verse 3 refers to an individual blessing of longevity and prosperity; others believe it's a collective promise for an entire nation. What do you think? Why?

5. What does it really mean to "honor" your mother? Describe with examples you've seen or heard about.

6. Is it appropriate for a Christian mother to demand to be honored by her children? Defend your answer.

Backseat Bible: *Ephesians 6:2*

The Greek verb translated "honor" in Ephesians 6:2 is *timaō* (a variant of the Greek word *time*). While *timaō* certainly includes the idea of "respect" as part of its definition, it's interesting to discover that the broader meaning of this word has to do with "value."

In fact, in Greek culture *timaō* was commonly used to refer to an "honorarium given for services rendered." What's more, in the New Testament, this same root word was used to describe the price received for selling land (Acts 4:34), the cost of Christ's redeeming work (1 Cor. 6:20), and the preciousness of Jesus's own blood (1 Pet. 1:19).[10]

Have group members read Philippians 4:8–9.

7. How might Philippians 4:8–9 be a helpful guide in our efforts to honor our mothers?

8. What part does gratefulness play in the expression of Philippians 4:8–9? And how does that influence a relationship between a child and a mother?

168

OPEN LIFE

9. It's likely that, at one time or another, your mother acted dishonorably or disappointed you. How does that affect your ability to value and respect her? What should be done about it?

10. What ideas do you have to help you live out the commands of Ephesians 6:2–3 and Philippians 4:8–9 this Mother's Day? Throughout the rest of this year?

Small Group Tip

Consider the option of having group members share their "Open Life" answers with a partner instead of with the whole group. This might be especially helpful if yours is a newly formed small group.

Afterward, have partners pray together in pairs to close the session.

47

memorial day

So David triumphed over the Philistine.

1 Samuel 17:50

THEME: **Heroes**

SCRIPTURE: *1 Samuel 17:41–50; Judges 6:11–24*

OPEN UP

(10–15 minutes)

1. You've been given the gift of one heroic superpower for twenty-four hours! What superpower do you choose, and why?

Small Group Tip: *For Extra Fun*

If your group is not easily embarrassed, have everyone act out their answers to question 1 charades-style! Give small prizes (such as a standing ovation or a comic book) to the crowd-pleasing superpower ideas and charades actors.

OPEN BOOK ▶

2. Memorial Day offers a great opportunity for us to remember—and be grateful for—heroes in our lives. What makes a hero? Explain it as you would to a child.

Have group members read 1 Samuel 17:41–50.

3. What comes to mind as you read this story of David's heroism and his confidence in God?

4. If God had not given David victory over Goliath, would David still be a hero in your eyes? Explain.

5. Finish this sentence: "For would-be heroes, the lesson of David and Goliath is . . ."

Backseat Bible: *1 Samuel 17:41–50*

In today's perspective, King Saul is sometimes viewed with disdain for allowing a boy, David, to fight Goliath instead of fighting the giant himself. However, within the culture and time that this event occurred, Saul's refusal of personal combat was the appropriate choice.

Because Saul was king of Israel, his lieutenants would have considered him far too important to risk in a hand-to-hand contest. Even if he had wanted to take Goliath's challenge, he likely would have been prevented from it by his inner circle. Additionally, at this time Saul was already beyond fighting age. Had he volunteered to fight Goliath, that action would have been seen as a clear insult to his troops—and an accusation that all his soldiers were cowards.[11]

Have group members read Judges 6:11–24.

6. What comes to mind as you read this story of Gideon's heroism and his lack of confidence in God?

7. Gideon felt abandoned by God (v. 13), yet he acted with heroic faith anyway. What makes that possible in a person?

171

8. Which is more significant: (a) that Gideon asked for signs of God's support, or (b) that God gave Gideon repeated signs of his support? Explain.

OPEN LIFE

(5–10 minutes)

9. What's one word that describes what the stories of David and Gideon communicate to you about God's heroic potential in your life? Explain your answer.

10. In honor of Memorial Day, you've been given the gift of performing one heroic act during the next week. What will you choose to do, and why?

Small Group Tip

Encourage group members to be specific in the way they answer "Open Life" questions. Also, instruct people to wait a minute or two in silence before answering. This will give them an opportunity to think through their responses a bit before having to talk.

48

juneteenth

He has sent me to proclaim freedom.

Luke 4:18

THEME: **Freedom**

SCRIPTURE: *Luke 4:16–21; John 8:34–36*

OPEN UP

(10–15 minutes)

1. June 19, 1865—over two years *after* President Lincoln's Emancipation Proclamation—Union soldiers finally landed in Galveston, Texas, and announced that all slaves in America were free. From then on, "Juneteenth," as it's been called, has been a cause for celebration nationwide.[12] If you could commemorate one day of your life as a celebration of freedom, what would it be? Why?

Small Group Tip

Because of the nature of a Bible study small group, many—or even all—may feel the "right" answer to give for question 1 is the date that they first became a Christian.

If this happens, first affirm everyone's choice. This is certainly an event worthy of celebration, so thank people for telling about it. Next, explain that you'll all be discussing more about freedom in Christ later in this session, and ask group members to think of another day in addition to "Salvation Day" that they could also commemorate as a celebration of freedom—religious or otherwise.

OPEN BOOK

(15–25 minutes)

2. It's often assumed that freedom is the innate desire of every person. Do you agree or disagree with that viewpoint? Defend your answer.

Have group members read Luke 4:16–21.

3. Exactly whom is Jesus talking about in this passage? And what relevance do his words have for us two thousand years later?

4. Many Christians today are poor, in captivity, blind, or oppressed. How does the harshness of these real-life situations influence what we understand about the freedom Christ promises in this Scripture?

5. On a practical, everyday level, how does the promise of Luke 4:18–19 show itself in our community here in the twenty-first century? Be specific, and be honest.

Backseat Bible: *Luke 4:16–21*

Jews at this time were familiar with the passage of Isaiah that Jesus read aloud in the synagogue—it was commonly considered to be a prophecy regarding the coming Messiah. That Jesus claimed fulfillment of the prophecy in himself meant he was also claiming to be the divine Messiah promised by Old Testament Scriptures.

This was a shocking assertion to make. In fact, his hearers were so enraged by it, they actually tried to murder him as a result (see Luke 4:28–30).[13]

Have group members read John 8:34–36.

6. In what ways does sin enslave a person? Think in terms of spiritual, emotional, physical, and relational impact.

7. Realistically speaking, how does Christ free us from sin?

8. Now, rewrite John 8:34–36 as if you were translating it for a five-year-old child. What would you say?

Small Group Tip

For question 8, consider having group members work to-gether in pairs or trios to come up with a few "translations" to share with the larger group.

OPEN LIFE

(5–10 minutes)

9. There are two kinds of freedom: "freedom from" and "freedom to." Which do you need most from Christ this week?

10. What will you do tomorrow to pursue that kind of freedom in him?

Small Group Tip

Encourage group members to be specific in the way they answer "Open Life" questions. Also, instruct people to wait a minute or two in silence before answering. This will give them an opportunity to think through their responses a bit before having to talk.

Small Group Tip

Consider the option of having group members share their "Open Life" answers with a partner instead of with the whole group. This might be especially helpful if yours is a newly formed small group.

Afterward, have partners pray together in pairs to close the session.

49

father's day

Love must be sincere.

Romans 12:9

THEME: **Fatherhood**

SCRIPTURE: *Colossians 3:19–21; Romans 12:9–18*

OPEN UP

(10–15 minutes)

1. In conjunction with Father's Day this year, we've been assigned to write a new runaway bestseller: *Father's Little Instruction Book*. What warm, pithy advice will we share in this upcoming masterpiece of philosophy and literature?

Small Group Tip: *For Extra Fun*

If possible, go ahead and record the advice and stories that people offer in response to questions 1 and 2. Afterward, compile them into a computer file and share it via email with everyone in your group.

OPEN BOOK

(15–25 minutes)

2. For Father's Day next year, our follow-up book will be titled *What My Dad Did Right*. What stories will we include in this surefire Pulitzer Prize winner?

Have group members read Colossians 3:19–21.

3. The apostle Paul never married or had children. Why do you suppose he felt obligated—and qualified—to tell fathers what was right?

4. How do the instructions of Colossians 3:19 affect a father's ability to follow the instruction of Colossians 3:21? A child's ability to follow the instructions of Colossians 3:20? Explain your answers.

5. Colossians 3:21 tells a father what not to do. What does that imply that a father *should* do? Be specific.

Backseat Bible: *Colossians 3:21*

In Jewish society of the biblical world, the father held almost limitless authority over his household (which could include wife, children, cousins, grandchildren, aunts, uncles, and other members of an extended family). Under that patriarchal system, a father ruled his family with the legal authority of a "little king"—including decisions over the life and death of family members.[14]

In that societal context, it must have been risky—and possibly offensive—for Paul to dare suggesting that a father temper his uncontested dominion over his children with concern for something as insignificant as their *feelings*!

Have group members read Romans 12:9–18.

6. What does this passage say to you about being a father to young children? About being a father to teenagers?

178

7. "Love must be sincere" (v. 9). When have you experienced the truth of that statement, either as a father or as the child of a father?

8. How and when do you notice your heavenly Father's expression of sincere love for you? What does that mean for your own father-child relationships?

OPEN LIFE

(5–10 minutes)

9. What's the most important thing you've discovered about fatherhood from today's discussion?

10. What's one way this discovery will have a positive effect on your life and relationships this week? Be specific.

Small Group Tip

Encourage group members to be specific in the way they answer "Open Life" questions. Also, instruct people to wait a minute or two in silence before answering. This will give them an opportunity to think through their responses a bit before having to talk.

50

halloween

Perfect love drives out fear.

1 John 4:18

THEME: **Fear**

SCRIPTURE: *Mark 4:35–41; Psalm 56:11; 2 Timothy 1:7; 1 John 4:18*

OPEN UP

(10–15 minutes)

1. What's the most unique phobia you've ever heard of? And have you ever known anyone with that fear? Tell about it.

Small Group Tip: *For Extra Fun*

If your group enjoys talking about eccentric phobias, and if time allows, go ahead and play the Phobia Game. Teams of two people each create an all-new, unique phobia—complete with symptoms and definitions—and present it to the group at large (skits optional!). The team with the most creative phobia wins!

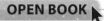 **OPEN BOOK**

(15–25 minutes)

2. Would you say that fear is a positive, negative, or neutral emotion? Defend your answer.

Have group members read Mark 4:35–41.

3. Fear has three main components: physical, spiritual, and psychological. How do you see fear at work in those areas in Mark 4:35–41?

4. God's presence was not enough to keep these disciples from experiencing fear. Why not?

5. How does faith combat fear?

6. Mark records that Jesus rescued his disciples from this storm—but Scripture also records histories of faithful believers who were *not* rescued from fearful situations (see Heb. 11:36–38). How does that affect the way you think about fear? Explain.

Backseat Bible: *Mark 4:37*

Even today, the Sea of Galilee experiences sudden, furious storms that threaten anything on the water. This is because it's located in a basin, encircled by mountains. The air at the bottom of the basin—where the sea is situated—tends to be warm and humid. Swirling, cool air from the Mediterranean frequently flows through the narrow mountain passes and crashes into that hot air at the bottom of the basin. The result? A "furious squall" can pop up almost any time.[15]

Have group members read Psalm 56:11; 2 Timothy 1:7; and 1 John 4:18.

7. What good are these Scriptures in the face of circumstances like war, unemployment, violent crime, serious illness, or any other of the scary situations we face in normal life?

8. What is God's responsibility when we are afraid? What is our responsibility?

OPEN LIFE (5–10 minutes)

9. Human beings appear to be the only species to exhibit a fear of the future. Why do you suppose that is?

10. At some point in the coming week, you are going to feel some measure of fear (worry, stress, anxiety, etc.). What advice would you like to give your future self about that situation?

Small Group Tip

Encourage group members to be specific in the way they answer "Open Life" questions. Also, instruct people to wait a minute or two in silence before answering. This will give them an opportunity to think through their responses a bit before having to talk.

51

thanksgiving

Give thanks in all circumstances.

1 Thessalonians 5:18

THEME: **Gratefulness**

SCRIPTURE: *1 Thessalonians 5:18; Luke 17:11–19*

OPEN UP

(10–15 minutes)

1. If you had to communicate gratefulness without speaking a word, what would you do? Show everyone right now.

OPEN BOOK

(15–25 minutes)

2. What makes it easy or difficult for you to feel grateful during the Thanksgiving holiday?

Have group members read 1 Thessalonians 5:18.

3. Why do you suppose it's God's will for us to be grateful?

4. What does a thankful lifestyle look like? Describe it.

5. Life hurts, and it's filled with disappointment. Doesn't it seem a little unreasonable to expect that we should be thankful in *all* circumstances? Why or why not?

Backseat Bible: *Luke 17:12–13*

While most theologians would not disagree with the idea that the cry, "Jesus, Master, have pity on us" (Luke 17:13) was a prayer for help, some scholars suggest that the lepers were not asking for a miracle—but for money. As societal outcasts, begging for alms was the only way they could gain basic necessities like food and clothing. In this view, Jesus heard their call for money and, instead, surprised them with a miracle of healing.[16]

If correct, this perspective might explain the spontaneous and joyful reaction of the one who returned (v. 15), and give a reason why the others didn't return. It also could have provided an example that Peter followed later, when a beggar asked him for alms in front of the temple (see Acts 3:1–10).

Have group members read Luke 17:11–19.

6. Which person in this story do you relate to most? Why?

7. Jesus never told the lepers they'd be healed, nor did he instruct them to give thanks after being healed—nor to do anything but go show themselves to the priest, which they did. So why did he seem disappointed when only one returned?

8. What benefits do you see in a lifestyle of gratefulness? And who is affected most by that lifestyle?

OPEN LIFE

(5–10 minutes)

9. If you were to communicate gratefulness to God in a different way each day this week, what might you do?

10. Which of those seven ideas will you dare to try out tomorrow?

Small Group Tip

For question 9, consider having group members work together in pairs or trios to brainstorm a few ideas to share with the entire group.

52

christmas

I bring you good news of great joy.

Luke 2:10

THEME: **Jesus's Birth**

SCRIPTURE: *Luke 2:1–20; John 3:16–17*

OPEN UP ➤

(10–15 minutes)

1. Close your eyes and try to picture the scene when Jesus was born. Using at least three of the five senses (sight, sound, smell, taste, and touch), describe what you see.

Small Group Tip: *For Extra Fun*

Word on the street is that this small group discussion guide goes great with spiced cider, gingerbread cookies, and maybe a jingle bell or two!

OPEN BOOK (15–25 minutes)

2. It's become controversial in America today to include Jesus in public celebrations of Christmas. How do you think Jesus would respond to that if he were with us physically this Christmas season?

Have group members read Luke 2:1–20.

3. What emotions do you feel as you read this account of Jesus's birth? Why?

4. Jesus's birth is cloaked in both abject humility (v. 7) and unmatched majesty (v. 13). What does that tell you about the nature of God—and about God's expectations for you?

5. If you could have spoken to Mary and Joseph just after Jesus's birth, what would you have said to them? Why?

Backseat Bible: *Luke 2:7–8*

Despite our snowy celebrations of Christmas, it's generally accepted as fact that Jesus was *not* born on December 25. In fact, it's unlikely he was born in winter at all, as is indicated by the presence of the shepherds in the nativity history. One theologian explains it this way:

> Bethlehem is intensely cold at the end of December, and no shepherds could have been "watching over their flocks by night" then. In the winter the flocks are taken into sheepfolds or caves at night, but in late summer sheep are too languid to feed in the daytime, so shepherds take them out at night. Everything points to the late summer or early autumn of 7 or 6 BC as the date of [Jesus's] birth.[17]

Have group members read John 3:16–17.

6. What kind of light does this famous Scripture shed on Luke 2:1–20?

7. Imagine that you could write a letter today that would be read by the ten-year-old version of you. If you were to

187

include a personal translation of John 3:16–17 in that letter, what would it say?

8. What does John 3:16–17 tell you about the nature of God—and about God's desire for you?

OPEN LIFE

(5–10 minutes)

9. Why does it matter that Jesus came to earth born as a baby—fully human, fully God, and free from sin?

10. What are you going to do about it this week?

Small Group Tip

Encourage group members to be specific in the way they answer "Open Life" questions. Also, instruct people to wait a minute or two in silence before answering. This will give them an opportunity to think through their responses a bit before having to talk.

appendix

Twenty Tips for Dynamic Discussions

1. Orchestrate, don't dominate.

Your job is not to place yourself center stage. Instead, like an orchestra conductor, your job is to prompt *others* to contribute to the chorus of conversation.

2. Challenge people to think beyond the obvious.

"Well, we should all just love Jesus more" is true . . . and it's a lazy, boring cop-out in any serious discussion of Scripture. So challenge your people to avoid easy, risk-free answers and to dig deeper—even if it means raising more questions!

3. Use follow-up cues.

If people are speaking only in vague generalities, try follow-up cues to help them get below the surface in their thinking. For instance: "Tell me more about that." "What do you mean?" "How would you explain that to a child?" "What else?" "Defend your answer." "Help me understand better what you're saying."

4. Be comfortable with silence.

Hey, it takes time to think about things that are important, so let your people have that time. Don't give in to the temptation to fill silences when thinking is occurring. Just wait for people to work through their thoughts. Somebody will speak up soon enough.

5. Remember, there's rarely one "right" answer.

Look, if this were a Bible quiz book then you could expect there to be a single "correct" answer to every question. But that's lower-order thinking. This book is all about getting people to move toward higher-order thinking about the Bible. That means anything's possible once a question is out there. Get used to it. You might like it.

6. Smile. Relax. Enjoy yourself.

I'm told that when a person is relaxed and happy, a smile is the innate response to seeing a friend. We all know this intuitively, so remember to smile as if you're actually glad to see the people in your group! It will help them—and you—relax and feel comfortable.

7. Be curious.

A friend of mine once told me that curiosity is the beginning of intimacy with God—and I think he's right. So in your discussions, let curiosity run amok. Feel free to chase a "rabbit trail" as long as it's an interesting one. Let your example of curiosity about God be one your group members imitate with enthusiasm!

8. Keep people safe from gossip.

Sometimes people in your small group will share personal information—possibly embarrassing or private things. Help everyone feel safe during sharing by regularly reminding people that what's shared in group stays in group (unless prohibited by law).

9. Encourage group members to ask questions.

A good small group discussion follows an outline—but never a script. Sometimes the questions you ask will prompt more questions from people in your group. That's OK—it shows they're thinking about the topic. So welcome relevant questions from group members . . . and sometimes even ask for them.

10. Don't be the Bible expert.

It's tempting at times to cut to the chase and say, "OK, here's what the Bible *really* means . . ." Avoid that temptation! It's much better for your group members to discover meaning themselves than for you to impose meaning that they are expected to accept.

11. Don't be the defining authority.

The questions in this book are fun. They're interesting. And they're *hard*. Sometimes your people will try to make them easier by asking you to redefine or clarify a portion of it. ("African or European swallow?") Don't take that responsibility. Challenge them to think through it instead by saying, "Define it however you think is best."

12. Pay attention to the place where you meet.

People who are physically uncomfortable soon become emotionally and intellectually uncomfortable. So if you have a choice, pick a meeting location that provides comfortable seating, noise level, temperature, and so on.

13. Mix things up from time to time.

As you work through the discussion guides, you'll soon discover that the order of the questions does follow a progression. However, that doesn't mean you have to ask every question in order. Feel free to adapt the questions and the question order to fit your group's interests and experience—and go ahead and add all-new questions of your own.

14. Watch the clock.

Be sensitive to the fact that your group members have other obligations. Always, *always* end on time. If it seems that time is running out, simply skip a few questions, skip to the end, or opt to pause the discussion and pick it up again at the next meeting.

15. Watch your people.

As discussions go, there will be times when one or two group members may begin to monopolize the time. Pay attention to who is talking, how much people are talking, and how people are responding to others who are talking. If necessary, direct attention to other, less aggressive group members to keep the group fluid and engaged.

16. Share responsibility for leadership.

One great thing about *Instant Small Group* is that anyone can lead. So, from time to time, go ahead and let someone else lead! Open your group, toss the book to a friend, and have that person take a turn facilitating discussion time. That kind of thing helps group camaraderie and confidence—and communicates value to your group members.

17. Don't be afraid to use pairs and trios.

Some discussions (such as brainstorming, personal life stories, or life application) simply work better when only two or three people are involved. So don't be afraid to occasionally have people find a partner to talk with about a question. After a few moments, you can have each pair share insights from their private discussion with everyone.

18. Pray. A lot.

The best discussion in the world is irrelevant if God is not at work. And the most innocuous conversation can change a person forever—if God is at work. So be sure to take time (before, during, after) to pray for God to be at work in your small group. You'll definitely notice the difference!

19. Trust. A lot.

It's hard to believe, but you're not responsible for the spiritual growth of your small group members. God is responsible for that (see 1 Cor. 3:6). Your job is to faithfully share God's Word—to "plant" and "water." So get your people talking about the Bible, and then get out of the way. Trust God to bring fruit out of your efforts.

20. Have fun!

Seriously, discovering God's Word in a small group should be a good time. So, you know, lighten up a little. Laugh a lot. Be grateful for the time God has given you with this group. Try out some of the "For Extra Fun" tips sprinkled throughout the book. And, well . . . have fun!

notes

Section 1 Discussion Guides about Christian Essentials

1. Craig S. Keener, *The IVP Bible Background Commentary: New Testament* (Downers Grove, IL: InterVarsity Press, 1993), 232.

2. "Caesarea Philippi." *Archaeological Study Bible* (Grand Rapids: Zondervan, 2005), 1589.

3. Warren W. Wiersbe, *The Bible Exposition Commentary, New Testament*, vol. 1 (Colorado Springs: Victor, 2001), 408.

4. Craig A. Evans, ed., *The Bible Knowledge Background Commentary, John's Gospel, Hebrews–Revelation* (Colorado Springs: Victor, 2005), 205.

5. Earl Radmacher, Ronald B. Allen, and H. Wayne House, eds., *Nelson's New Illustrated Bible Commentary* (Nashville: Thomas Nelson, 1999), 728.

6. John F. Walvoord and Roy B. Zuck, *The Bible Knowledge Commentary, Old Testament* (Colorado Springs: Victor Books, 1985), 28.

7. Craig A. Evans, ed., *The Bible Knowledge Background Commentary, Acts–Philemon* (Colorado Springs: Victor, 2004), 200, 218.

8. Keener, *Bible Background Commentary: New Testament*, 99.

9. *ESV Study Bible* (Wheaton, IL: Crossway Bibles, 2008), 2071.

10. Keener, *Bible Background Commentary: New Testament*, 544.

11. Radmacher, Allen, and House, *Illustrated Bible Commentary*, 1151.

12. John F. Walvoord and Roy B. Zuck, *The Bible Knowledge Commentary, New Testament* (Colorado Springs: Victor Books, 1983), 708.

13. Lawrence O. Richards, *Expository Dictionary of Bible Words* (Grand Rapids: Regency Reference Library/Zondervan, 1985), 496.

14. Keener, *Bible Background Commentary: New Testament*, 246–47.

Section 2 Discussion Guides about Personal Growth

1. Michael L. Lindvall, *What Did Jesus Do?* (New York: Sterling Publishing, 2006), 51.

2. F. F. Bruce, *The International Bible Commentary* (Grand Rapids: Marshall Pickering/Zondervan, 1986), 1330.

3. *Archaeological Study Bible* (Grand Rapids: Zondervan, 2005), 1608.

4. Keener, *Bible Background Commentary: New Testament*, 117.

5. *Archaeological Study Bible*, 1608.   ·

6. *ESV Study Bible*, 1487.

7. Ibid., 970.

8. Richards, *Expository Dictionary*, 363.

9. Walvoord and Zuck, *Bible Knowledge Commentary, New Testament*, 708.

10. Richards, *Expository Dictionary*, 362.

11. Keener, *Bible Background Commentary: New Testament*, 620.

12. Ibid.

13. Don Campbell, Wendell Johnston, John Walvoord, and John Witmer, *The Theological Wordbook* (Nashville: Word/Thomas Nelson, 2000), 262–64.

14. Samuel Bagster, *Bagster's Bible Handbook* (Old Tappan, NJ: Fleming H. Revell, 1983), 128.

15. Miriam Feinberg Vamosh, *Daily Life at the Time of Jesus* (St. Louis, MO: Concordia, 2007), 29. See also Ralph Gower, *The New Manners and Customs of Bible Times* (Chicago: Moody, 1987), 256–58.

16. "Syria/Aram," *Archaeological Study Bible*, 534.

17. Merrill C. Tenney, *New Testament Survey* (Grand Rapids: Eerdmans, 1961), 188–89.

18. Wayne A. Detzler, *New Testament Words in Today's Language* (Wheaton, IL: Victor Books/SP Publications, 1986), 174.

19. Campbell, et al., *Theological Wordbook*, 135.

20. Mark Bailey and Tom Constable, *The New Testament Explorer* (Nashville: Word/Thomas Nelson, 1999), 390.

21. Walvoord and Zuck, *Bible Knowledge Commentary, New Testament*, 305.

Section 3 Discussion Guides about Family and Community

1. C. S. Mann, ed., *Mark*, vol. 27, *The Anchor Bible* (Garden City, NY: Doubleday, 1986), 396.

2. *The Interpreter's Bible*, vol. 4 (Nashville: Abingdon Press, 1955), 802.

3. Markus Barth, ed., *Ephesians 4–6*, vol. 34a, *The Anchor Bible* (Garden City, NY: Doubleday, 1974), 518.

4. Joseph A. Fitzmyer, ed., *The Gospel According to Luke 10–24*, vol. 28a, *The Anchor Bible* (Garden City, NY: Doubleday, 1985), 883.

5. Frederick Carl Eiselen, Edwin Lewis, and David G. Downey, eds., *The Abingdon Bible Commentary* (Nashville: Abingdon, 1929), 1043.

6. Kenneth L. Chafin, *The Communicator's Commentary: 1, 2 Corinthians*, Lloyd J. Ogilvie, ed. (Waco, TX: Word, 1985), 160–61.

7. *The Interpreter's Bible*, vol. 2 (Nashville: Abingdon, 1955), 373, 375.

8. *ESV Study Bible*, 182, 1870.

9. *The Interpreter's Bible*, vol. 9 (Nashville: Abingdon, 1955), 197–98.

10. Walvoord and Zuck, *Bible Knowledge Commentary, New Testament*, 847.

11. Charles R. Swindoll, *Insights on James, 1 & 2 Peter* (Grand Rapids: Zondervan, 2010), 178, 180.

12. Harold L. Wilmington, *Wilmington's Bible Handbook* (Wheaton, IL: Tyndale, 1997), 617.

13. Mann, *Mark*, 282–83.

14. *ESV Study Bible*, 2272–73.

Section 4 Discussion Guides about Holidays

1. Keener, *Bible Background Commentary: New Testament*, 270.

2. Eiselen et al., *Abingdon Bible Commentary*, 526.

3. Mitchell Dahood, ed., *Psalms 1 (1–50)*, vol. 16, *The Anchor Bible* (Garden City, NY: Doubleday, 1966), 146.

4. Wiersbe, *Bible Exposition Commentary, New Testament*, 602.

5. *The Interpreter's Bible*, vol. 10 (Nashville: Abingdon, 1955), 76–77.

6. Gail Gibbons, *St. Patrick's Day* (New York: Holiday House, 1994), 7, 8, 13, 27.

7. Keener, *Bible Background Commentary: New Testament*, 632.

8. Gary W. Demarest, *The Communicator's Commentary: 1, 2 Thessalonians, 1, 2 Timothy, Titus*, Lloyd J. Ogilvie, ed. (Waco, TX: Word, 1984), 294.

9. J. R. Porter, *Jesus Christ* (New York/Oxford: Oxford University Press, 1999), 129.

197

10. Detzler, *New Testament Words*, 216.

11. Alfred J. Hoerth, *Archaeology and the Old Testament* (Grand Rapids: Baker Books, 1998), 255.

12. "History of Juneteenth," accessed January 8, 2010, http://www .juneteenth.com/history.htm. 1996–2009.

13. *ESV Study Bible*, 1956–58.

14. Gower, *New Manners and Customs*, 57.

15. *Archaeological Study Bible*, 1633.

16. Fitzmyer, *Luke*, 1154.

17. Eiselen et al., *Abingdon Bible Commentary*, 1034.

scripture index

theme index

about the author

Mike Nappa is a bestselling and award-winning author and editor of many books, ministry resources, and magazine articles. He holds a master's degree in English and a bachelor's degree in Christian Education with an emphasis in Bible theology.

You can learn more about Mike at www.Nappaland.com.